Pumpkin

Caroline Anne Butt

Pumpkin

Pumpkin
ISBN 978 1 76041 697 3
Copyright © Caroline Anne Butt 2019
Cover: *Pumpkin Girl*, E.J. Wilson

First published 2019 by
Ginninderra Press
PO Box 3461 Port Adelaide 5015
www.ginninderrapress.com.au

Contents

Preface		7
1	The Iron Age	9
2	A Step at a Time	17
3	Home Away From Home	20
4	More Than Their Penny's Worth	23
5	68 Penshurst Street	30
6	The Arts	35
7	Kings and Queens	40
8	New Neighbours	44
9	Keeper of the Watch	46
10	Margot Fonteyn	49
11	A Beloved Room-mate	51
12	A Social Embarrassment	56
13	Cremorne Girls High	59
14	Infinite Questions	65
15	Turning Fourteen	70
16	School by the Beach	77
17	Banyandah	80
18	Spring	84
19	First Date	92
20	The Change	96
21	Punch-drunk	99
22	Twenty Per Cent Discount	103
23	Girl Space	109
24	Kadinsky	114
25	IBM Was in Town	116

26	Amazing Love	118
27	Who'd Want to Marry Her?	120
28	Last Chance	122
29	'I Saw Tomorrow –'	125
30	Thanks, Dad	129
31	Hazelbrook	132
32	The Novocastrian	136
33	Philip Baxter	142
34	Darwin and Central Australia	145
35	A Man and a Woman	152
36	The Perfect Companion	155
37	Southern Highlands	159
38	A Necessary Education	164
39	A Troublesome Attitude	167
40	For Better or for Worse	176
41	Snail Mail	184
42	For Two Years –	191
43	Pumpkin Dreams	194
44	The First Smile	202
45	The Wings of a Dove	207
46	Lateral Thinking	212
47	CVA	214
48	A Solitary Nature	219
49	White Roses	224
50	A Real Gem	230
51	Milk Tides	232
	Family History and Influences	237

Preface

When we lived in Mount Victoria in the Blue Mountains, I attended a life writing course run by Patti Miller at Varuna, Katoomba, in 1995. By that time, I'd had some life writing pieces published.

The course required a finished five-thousand-word piece. When finished, both my children, Paul and Rebecca, read it at different times, and at different ages, yet they had identical responses. Each put an arm around me. 'Mum, I want to know more. You have to write more.'

I never had any intention of going down the life writing path. At the time, I was writing for children and I was cautious about life writing because of inherent issues. How do you tell your story, which involves others, while respecting their story, which is theirs to tell? What form should it take? Autobiography? Family history? Memoir?

I chose memoir. I've been able to follow a single thread, in this instance of a young girl's point of view as she grows into a woman, in changing social and cultural times. On and off, it's taken twenty-one years to write and has finally come of age. Time to stand on its own two feet.

1
The Iron Age

17th August Anne born at 5.55 a.m. both well. Old man took fit when he heard it was a girl also Gran took one too. worse in fact then the old man forgot to get Stan his brekky. tough luck.

This note is the draft of a telegram Stan sent to his mother on the day of my birth. Ruby found it soon after he died. It was among personal papers in the top drawer of his lowboy. It was more in character for Ruby to throw non-useful things away but she kept this note and gave it to me not long before she died. 'I know you'll appreciate this,' she said. And I do.

Everyone knew that 'the old man', Stan, and Ruby, his 'cheese-n-kisses' were hoping for a girl this time.

On receiving the telegram, his mother rang him from a neighbour's phone. 'Congratulations. How are they?'

'Pretty good, considering.'

'Considering?'

'Something's missing.'
'Oh, dear, no. What?'
'Hasn't got a spout.'
'Oh, Stan. Don't frighten your poor old mother like that.'

Whenever Nanna told this story, it sounded like she was still in Recovery.

World War II had been declared in Europe in 1939. The nation was filled with dread. On 8 December 1941, Australian Prime Minister John Curtin declared, 'Men and women of Australia, we are at war with Japan.' Three years later, in 1944, there was good news. On D-Day, 6 June, there were reports that the Allies had landed in France and were gaining ground. Germany was in retreat. Prime Minister Curtin cautioned the nation, 'The war will not end in the Pacific until the Australian prisoners of war are released.'

At 68 Penshurst Street, Willoughby, loved ones fought their own front line of dread and uncertainty. Many an unwelcome telegram had arrived. Young William Hatton killed in action. William Thompson and Arthur Butt missing in action. The family was unaware that they'd been captured by the Japanese and were prisoners of war, working on the barbarous Burma–Thailand Railway. Everyone kept their eyes on the distant hopeful horizon.

At the first burst of freesias, Ruby knew her third child's birth was imminent. 'I remember when the first freesia came out. It was just before you were born. It was a little bit of light in all that darkness.'

While my arrival was a source of delight for some, the thought of it overwhelmed thirty-year-old Ruby. 'It couldn't have happened at a worse time. For the past six weeks, I'd had Uncle Mick and Gran sick with pleurisy and pneumonia.'

I was delivered by Doctor Storman on Thursday 17 August 1944 at the Mater Misericordiae Maternity Hospital, Wollstoncraft, North Sydney.

Stan announced to all, 'Baby born at the crack of dawn.'

Ruby had been puzzled by her high energy during the pregnancy. She ran an efficient and busy household and surprised herself. 'I was digging, gardening, knitting, more than usual yet I didn't know how I was going to cope.'

The thought of Ruby not coping was unthinkable. My mother was equal to God. She could move mountains if so inclined. On the due date, there were no expected labour pains. It didn't help matters that both my brothers had arrived on time.

Ruby took the matter into her own hands. The front veranda needed a good scrub. She thought that might bring on labour, so she got down on her hands and knees and scrubbed the tiles. But, still, there were no twinges. 'I thought I'll fix you. I don't have time to play games.'

At this point in my life, I was completely unaware of the poor impression I was making on my mother. Life could've been so much easier, for both of us, had I known, preferably while still in the womb.

Ruby decided to paint the front veranda. 'I thought that might get things moving. It was something I'd been meaning to do. You should have seen my tummy hanging over the tiles, almost touching the wet paint.'

'What colour?'

'Burgundy.'

Of course. Ruby was pure burgundy.

'You thought you were coming in your own sweet time but you had another think coming, don't you worry. I knew a lot about you already.'

Ruby believed that by the time each child was born she had their measure. She said that our behaviour in the womb indicated attitude, personality and character.

'I still don't know how you happened.'

'So, you didn't want me?'

'That's not a nice thing to say or even think.'

'Mum, I'm joking.' I was ignorant at this stage. I didn't know you couldn't joke with Ruby about whether a baby was wanted or not. In fact, I was ignorant of many things. It'd be decades before Ruby answered a lifelong question: 'Mum, what was the real reason I wore irons?'

I was fifty-five before Ruby could be encouraged to tell me, reluctant syllable by reluctant syllable. It had to be dragged out of her resistance. But I needed to know. Did it have anything to do with my one-day-overdue arrival on planet Earth?

Both Robert and Lennie had walked by the time they were twelve months old. By twelve months, I was supposedly quite speedy, skimming around the floor on my bottom. It began to look less and less likely that I'd walk. My earliest memory of trying to stand is before I wore plaster boots, then irons.

I pull myself up and cling to the edge of the table. I can see over the top. A pat of yellow butter sits in the middle of the table. The tablecloth slips. My legs buckle. Someone swoops me up. I'm in their arms and can see the top of the table as if for the first time. I see knives, forks, spoons, bread and butter plates, cups and saucers, teaspoons, all set in the same way. I recognise there's a significance to the setting of the table; my first awareness of patterns, family patterns and rituals.

Ruby followed her instincts and took me to see the family doctor, known to be a good diagnostician. He'd get her daughter walking. The young mother believed the problem was more than likely a case of inherited weak ankles and high insteps. Stan's high insteps had kept him out of the armed forces.

The doctor diagnosed mild cerebral palsy (CP). He immediately referred me to a Macquarie Street specialist. Ruby hoped that the doctor was wrong.

As a busy young mother, Ruby rarely had time to shop so she and her sister-in-law decided to do some serious window-shopping while in town after the specialist's appointment. But the Macquarie specialist confirmed mild cerebral palsy. B was sworn to secrecy. Apart from Stan, from henceforth, all inquisitors, including close family, friends and all future medics, were told, 'Anne wears irons because she has weak ankles like her father.'

The conscientious young mother was determined to gift her daughter the same upbringing as her sons. Also, she carried a secret fear. In her eighties, she said to me, 'I've often wondered if those tablets I had to take when I didn't know I was –'

'Mum, look at me. I'm fine. It wasn't your fault.'

She'd give me half a nod but carried its emotional weight and a degree of guilt for the rest of her life.

Both Stan and Ruby attended the next specialist appointment. The specialist explained the need to operate. Small sections of bone needed to be cut out of each foot. He'd perform the surgery at a private hospital in Double Bay.

The troubled parents said they needed more time to think about it. While they had private health insurance with the Railways and Tramways Health Fund, they worried that the risks were too great. 'It seemed unnatural to be cutting out bone.'

On their next visit, they asked about the alternatives. They soon realised they weren't meant to question the elegant, six-foot-two, navy blue pinstriped authority.

The alternative was for me to wear plaster boots for six months and callipers for an indefinite period. Ruby said at that point they were quickly ushered out of the specialist's rooms. 'I don't handle those cases in my rooms. You'll have to see me at Outpatients at the Royal [Royal North Shore Hospital, RNSH].'

I was put into plaster boots under a light anaesthetic at fourteen months. Each boot weighed three-quarters of a pound.

Stan's eyes would fill at the very mention. 'Bloody cruel, if you ask me. Wasn't like the boots fitted you for six months, either.'

No memory of plaster boots. Was there a new pair moulded every couple of months? I don't know but, whenever there is the slightest whiff of ether, I have to suppress an instinctive urge to flee.

After six months, I was fitted with irons and my mother and I began our demanding trek to and from RNSH, which also meant a change in family routine. Robert and Lennie would stay at home with Gran on those occasions until they were old enough to go to school.

Around this time, Stan bought a 1928 Dodge and, when he had a day off work, he'd drive us to and from hospital. Mostly, though, we caught a tram at Mowbray Road and alighted at the busy Crows Nest junction. Ruby would have to push the stroller across rows of tramlines, perfect traps for small stroller wheels.

After waiting hours, junior doctors would measure and check callipers and adjust them according to progress. Once a month, the specialist checked them. He'd write out a prescription for alterations to be made to the boots then we'd go across to the bootmaker. The smell of leather and glue was intoxicating. Back to hospital. Wait for specialist to check adjustments.

'And you had to have two drops of fish oil every morning and night. Very expensive it was. A small bottle cost five pounds.'

The most important part of the treatment was the most difficult. Bare feet were not allowed to touch the ground under any circumstances. I was not allowed out of bed until someone came and put on my special shoes and irons. Parents were warned that if they ignored this instruction they could set back their child's progress for months, even years.

Understandably, some parents couldn't do it. When down at the beach, or on holidays, they couldn't resist letting their child feel the sand between their toes. They let them paddle in the cool rock pools. As a result, there'd be the inevitable relapse and the parent would feel the full ire of the specialist.

'Sometimes we'd hear him shouting at them and we'd shudder. They'd come out wiping their eyes or blowing their nose. It was awful.'

This was a risk Ruby and Stan were not prepared to take; not when catching-up-with-rellies-weekends-away at Hazelbrook or Yass or on our annual month-long beach holidays. I never felt the sand or salt water between my toes until the irons were removed.

When on the beach someone would keep me busy making sandcastles. We'd decorate them with shells and small sticks. Everyone helped tip buckets of water into the deep moats dug around the castles. With small sticks, I could draw shells, rocks, waves and people.

I still feel a delicious thrill when paddling and/or skipping like Dorothy along the water's edge, singing, 'We're off to see the Wizard…' It's a song of praise for the privilege.

It was always difficult to get Ruby to talk about this time. Even in her eighties she still seemed somewhat traumatised. After all, she was the one who sat in the waiting room fully conscious of the seriousness of many of the difficult cases around her. Parents shared their hopes and sorrows as they sat there. And Ruby, always a sympathetic, non-judgemental listener, listened. People gravitated to her to tell their stories. She said she coped by knitting.

In her eighties, when she finally answered my question about why I wore irons, Ruby was still knitting and listening but by now she was far enough away from Outpatients at RNSH to talk. 'It was all those sad stories…those crippled children…parents' hopes crushed. I was determined to get you out of irons as soon as I could. I wanted you out of them before you went to school. That was my aim, you know. I think it's why I had such a bad time during the Change. I was too busy before then to think about it. I've learnt that worrying doesn't change a thing.'

As a child, I was oblivious to this dimension. I don't remember any trauma associated with it, although I was always anxious about something. When we waited at the hospital, I was anxious about slippery floors; anxious about men dressed in coats who came through big double doors. They'd be wheeling someone down the corridor in a big bed. 'Where are they going, Mummy?'

'To see a doctor. Don't stare. It's rude.'

But I needed to stare. I was worried the person lying on the bed might be dead.

Sitting in Outpatients was like sitting in a mustard-coloured worry world compared to the bright blue and green world outside. Apart from sitting there, watching nurses hurry about, whisper-quiet, in and out of small cubicles, I'd sometimes catch the eye of a child, nearby, in a wheelchair. And I'd wonder. Why is he dribbling? Grunting? Limbs jumping? I'd smile back but I wasn't allowed to talk to strangers so would sit close to Mummy and watch her knit.

One day, the specialist gave Ruby good news. 'She should be out of these sometime in the next twelve months.'

Ruby could afford to dream now. 'I only had to think about having another little girl and I was expecting.'

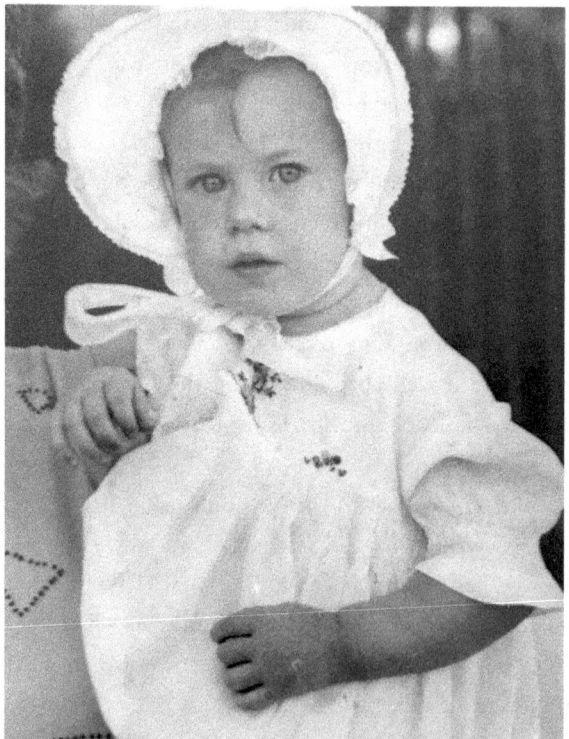

Anne.

2
A Step at a Time

When Wendy Ruby was born on her due date, 29 November 1948, Penshurst Street was still a busy family hub. It was always house full.

A day or two after she was born, Stan took me to the Mater Maternity Hospital to choose a new baby sister. In those days, children weren't allowed to visit their mothers in maternity wards. We were going to meet Mummy at the nursery.

When we got out of the lift, she was standing there by the nursery's big viewing window. Mummy was in a nightie and brunch coat. She looked and smelt different. We looked at the babies. Sister wheeled one particular crib up to the window, right in front of me. This baby was beautiful. Dark, curly hair. Yes, this was the one and everyone smiled. We were all very happy until it was time to leave.

Mummy said she had to get the new baby ready to bring home, the truth being Ruby had so many stitches it was too uncomfortable for her to stand for very long.

About ten days later, mother and baby arrived home. Shortly after, they discovered the baby missing. She was soon found, not too far away, in the next room, in her little big sister's arms, being swayed and cooed. Afraid I might drop her, it's said Ruby crept in, as if very calm, and suggested we put the baby back to bed so she could have a sleep. Apparently, putting the baby down was quite a team effort because I didn't want to let go.

Wendy is a few weeks old. She's just had a bath in the metal baby's bath. She lies on her tummy on a white towel laid out on the kitchen table. The kitchen walls are the colour of early morning sunshine. The sun glows into the kitchen. It shines on baby. I sprinkle silky Johnson's baby powder all over baby's back. Mummy and I pat it in.

Mummy says, 'Smooth as a baby's bottom,' and we laugh.

While Mummy dries my little sister, I wash Baby Doll in the baby's bath.

In the spring of 1949, my irons were removed. I was just a few weeks shy of starting school. Ruby had moved mountains again. Before we left the building, I'm sure there were fond farewells and good wishes from the regular troopers in the waiting room.

We're walking out of the building. I'm holding Mummy's hand. She's walking too fast. We walk onto the wooden ramp which joins two buildings. I freeze. There are gaps between the boards. Never seen them before. I peer down. The sun is on the ground lying down there in pieces. I look at my feet, afraid I might fall through. Can't move.

In the meantime, I imagine Ruby's feet should've been well above ground. The sheer momentum of the occasion should've had her dancing, but, instead, she was standing still, holding the hand of a terrified child. Couldn't move. We'd walked back and forth across this ramp for years but this was the first time without irons. My new-found, newly grounded independence was quickly coming unstuck.

Mummy says, 'I'll take a step. See?'

I look at her foot. It's not falling through. I take one big step, over the first gap. Don't fall through.

Mummy says, 'Now, one more…and another… See, it's easy…one step at a time.'

Just one step at a time. That was how my mother enabled me to reach the other side of terror. Understandably, there were many false starts which I don't remember.

Apparently, I cried for months wanting my irons. I started to wet the bed. Fell over and over, skinning knees, elbows, palms. Fell up and down stairs. Crashed into walls and doors. Already quite the tomboy who tried to keep up with my active, sporty brothers, I managed to break both wrists twice and collarbone. I was always falling onto some current knee and elbow wound. Sometimes, my weeping wounds were so badly re-grazed that the local nurse had to dress them. It was during these clumsy, action-filled days that I learnt to stand on my own two feet.

Stan and Ruby, 1941.

3
Home Away From Home

It's my first day at school and Mummy wants to take me. I tell her no. I want to run ahead with the boys but she says, 'No. Hold onto the stroller and walk, properly, like a young lady.'

Meanwhile, Robert and Lennie run ahead and disappear through the gates of Willoughby Boys. My inside legs are flying but, in reality, it seems like we're hardly moving.

As soon as we reach the Infants' gate, I turn to kiss Mummy but she pushes the stroller through. I want to go in on my own but she says, 'If I don't come with you on your very first day, the teacher will think I'm a terrible mother… Sit here and wait for your name to be called.'

Didn't know I had to wait for my name to be called and I don't want the teacher to think my mummy is terrible. We sit in a corner of the quadrangle on a long wooden seat in the cool morning shade of the two-storey brick building.

It'll be fun in Mrs P's class. Robert and Lennie were in her class. Everyone loves Mrs P. She's like Mrs Hughes, next door. She has a sunshine face, apricot hair and kind eyes. A bell rings and there's Mrs P standing at the door. She calls our names and smiles.

Kindergarten has two large rooms with concertina doors pushed right back. We're allowed to play wherever we want. One side of the room is full of light and there's a dolly's and dress-up corner and a small kitchen. On the other side of the room there are some small tables and chairs just like the ones we have at Sunday school and very different to the hospital ones.

Pencils and crayons are like magnets to me. I sit down on my own and pick up a crayon and start drawing on some paper. From here, I can see outside. Mummy is still standing outside the school gate. She's rolling the stroller backwards and forwards, backwards and forwards, while she talks to another mother. They're smiling and laughing, which makes me feel even happier, if that's possible. All is right in my bright new world. I will sit in this seat forever.

After lunch, Mrs P calls me over and tells me how lucky I am because I'm going to Mrs E's class, Transition. I know it isn't fair. It's a big mistake but I mustn't cry. A couple of us follow a lady out of the buttercup Kindy room to a room far away, along a dark corridor to the very end. Mrs E greets us and says to come in and sit down on the mats. We sit in front of the big children. There's no dolly's corner, no dress-ups, no toys, only afternoon glare coming through big windows. Rows of desks fill most of the space except for the big mats which have been rolled out in front of the blackboard where everyone sits. On either side of the blackboard are low bookcases filled with books all the same colour and size. Why are there so many books the same? I discover they're called Readers.

I learn to read by osmosis, quite unaware of the process. Before going to school, we'd learnt to recite the alphabet backwards and forwards because it's one of our family games. Daddy times us. He also runs spelling bees while sitting around the dining table or when we're travelling long distances.

At school, we read aloud every day. It's important not to lose your place when someone else is reading. It's my turn. I've lost my place. Want to cry. Mrs E finds the place. It's pages back. Unknowingly, I'd fallen headlong into story. Real reading: a firework within; a bursting forth of self.

On Friday afternoons, we dance and sing and play music with Kindergarten. Outside, large classes of forty, fifty, sixty children form a big circle. The circle is so big it takes up most of second class playground. We sing 'Farmer in the Dell', time and time again.

We also play musical instruments. Playing the cymbals at my first school concert was my first experience of stage fright. Will my arms move in time to the beat? Special clanging times are a worry but my arms seem to have a well-rehearsed mind of their own. The band is exciting. It gives me a free ticket into another world. There's sound, rhythm, doh, ray, me, 1, 2, 3. I discover they're patterns too. I'm learning how to read them. They're called music.

*

Time

I might have said
let me begin
at the end
but
time ran away
and
chased its tail
till
there was
no beginning
no end
just time rolling by.

4
More Than Their Penny's Worth

With irons removed, my independence grew out of bounds. I'd recently overheard my mother say that she had 'too many mouths to feed and too many beds to make'. Whatever I overheard, it must've left me with the impression that my mother needed a rest.

If Lennie and I could go and stay at Aunty Jean's, just down the road, then there'd be less to do. Aunty Jean would think it was a very good idea. She'd ring Mummy and tell her that we could stay there for a while. Somehow, I convinced my older brother, Lennie, to come with me. We packed my tiny blue port. It was said to contain a pair of pyjamas, underpants for Lennie and one white sock.

We planned to leave early in the morning. We only had about eight blocks to walk. Our biggest obstacle was how to cross busy Mowbray Road, so we stood on the corner of Mowbray and Penshurst Streets and waited for a big person to put us across. A tram slowed down at the stop and a man jumped off and walked towards us. He waved. It was Uncle Bill. He'd recently moved out of 68 to a neighbouring suburb only a short tram ride away.

This was perfect. He'd help us across Mowbray Road. We told him our plan. He suggested that first of all we come back with him because he was pretty sure there'd be a big, hot pot of porridge on the stove by now. Who could resist hot porridge and brown sugar?

A few years later I plan a more serious run-away. This one I hope to be Famous Five Enid Blyton style. I'm nine or ten, standing in the kitchen asking my mother if I can play. My brothers are off playing with friends. Ruby is sprinkling water onto hankies and pillowcases, rolling them tight, so tight they squeal. She heats the heavy iron on the hot resting plate. She tests the iron by lightly touching the bottom of it with the wet tip of her finger, It hisses. Hot enough. 'I want you to iron these before you go.'

I plead with her to let me go and play. 'Why don't the boys have to iron? Not fair…' I rant on behalf of all girls who've ever had to iron and whose brothers didn't.

'It's what girls do. I ironed at your age.'

'Why? Why do only girls iron?' I flounce about and threaten to run away because it isn't fair.

I'm slapped on the side of the face. I've never been slapped before. Never ranted like that before either. I'm speechless – well, not quite. 'You – you just hit me.'

'I shouldn't have. I'm very sorry. But wake up to yourself.'

'I was just saying, that's all.'

'Get inside. Out of my sight.'

I hide my delicious pleasure at being sent to my room. It's so quiet in here. Besides, it gives me time to plan. If I run away, the boys will have to iron. I'll live next door in Mr Hughes's big shed on the mezzanine floor. I'd coveted it for years. It would make an ideal cubby house. No one will look for me there. They'll think I've run away to another country. I'll stay in the shed until everyone's in bed. I'll still be close to our outside toilet and bathroom and close to the kitchen pantry. In the silence of my bedroom, I vow never to speak to my mother, ever again.

There's a knock on the bedroom door. Ruby opens it. 'You can come out now. I've put the kettle on.'

We sit at the kitchen table. I'm quieter. Ruby seems brighter. We eat Jatz and cheese and drink Kinkara tea and we talk about anything but the earlier rupture.

We had significant disagreements when I was in high school. I was often halfway to the bus stop before remembering I wasn't supposed to be talking to my mother but I would've already kissed her goodbye and waved as she stood on the front veranda as she did every morning, waving to us, each in our turn, until out of sight.

Disagreements were mostly about what was expected of girls and what was not expected of boys. I'd point out that the expectations were so unfair. Ruby would turn away. There'd be a chill, the same sort of feeling when the sun goes behind the clouds. Complete disengagement. I couldn't afford this. I never wanted to displease my mother. She was the very air I breathed.

Ruby had high expectations. She had so much to teach her daughter on the domestic front. No one could make a bed like Ruby, except perhaps Matron or someone in the armed forces. Every day, every bed would be stripped, sheets and blankets shaken then put back on with absolute precision and crisp hospital corners. Monday morning. Bed linen changed. Sheets and pillowcases washed, pillowcases starched. A sweet fragrance of fresh linen would greet us every Monday night as we climbed into bed. It was Ruby's blessing to the whole family; her love offering.

At night, after we'd finish washing up, we'd climb into our pjs and go to bed.

Ruby would call out, 'We'll be in in a minute,' which meant we could talk or read until lights out.

Soon they'd be there; a visual benediction standing at the end of our beds.

Stan would pretend to tuck us in more tightly, deliberately rocking the side of the bed as he did so. 'Just want to make sure you don't fall out.'

We'd giggle at his nonsense then there'd be more goodnights, lights out and we'd listen for the middle door to close. At times, I went to bed with some girl-injustice niggling away at me but with the nighty-night ritual it soon dissipated. Wendy and I would whisper until she fell asleep. Then it was time to take out my torch from under the bed and open the latest book. There was always a torch under our beds because we sometimes needed to use the potty in our parents' bedroom during the night.

Usually I was lost in some Enid Blyton adventure and didn't hear Ruby open the middle door. 'Put that book away and go to sleep.'

It took me a while to work out how she knew I was reading. It was the dim glow reflecting off the wardrobe mirror opposite the end of the bed.

Holding the torch under the blankets, halfway down the bed, because there was always another page to read, didn't work either but, in time, there was an unspoken truce.

At first, Gran doubted I read books quickly. One Christmas she gave me an Enid Blyton's Famous Five which I devoured during Christmas celebrations on Christmas Day.

Next morning, Boxing Day, I was looking for something to do and Gran suggested I read my new book. When I said I'd read it, she looked dubious. 'Go and get it.'

I already felt guilty for having read it on Christmas Day when I'd been told by my mother, several times, to put the book away and go outside and play.

Gran questioned me on the characters and storyline. 'All right, but you might as well read it again, make sure we get our penny's worth.'

Little did Gran know my intention was to reread it many times. Books were always worth more than their penny's worth.

The King James Holy Bible was part of my bedtime reading almost every day during the late primary and teen years. I was a member of the Scripture Union (SU).

A small SU cardboard calendar was folded up and kept inside the front cover of the Bible. Each day there were designated verses to read. Some readings were incomprehensible; nonetheless, the verses fed a hungry spirit which could sup on tasty metaphors and feed on the miracle of miracles.

Some Sundays in church we chanted eagle-winged, stained-glass, leather-bound Psalms. Sometimes, I knelt with others, feeding marrow and spirit in the respectful morning light, heads bowed. Quiet. Being as one.

In my teens, I could afford to pay for accompanying Scripture Union notes which had a commentary on the daily reading, and often their long bow of interpretation made me wonder if one was allowed to disagree with them. At this stage, I started an instinctive journal, narrowing the focus with an increasing need to tell the white pages about the circling, startling eagles of thought. The journal was private and listened in the quiet of my room. It became a source of light, the beginning of heady times, sometimes sought morning and night.

Writing times provided private audiences with God where issues could be raised. For example, Lot's wife. She needed an advocate. The journal contained persuasive arguments on her behalf. Surely, most people would've turned around, so why turn her into a pillar of salt?

Why ask Abraham to be prepared to sacrifice his son just to show he loved you more? How scary was that! Abraham loved his son. Wasn't that enough? Love in our home was always gentle and kind. Why so much cruelty?

From the pulpit, we were taught not to question God's word; exhorted to ignore our feelings. They were unreliable, transitory. These teachings were confusing. Didn't our feelings tell us things? And how could you not ask questions?

The journal became a crucial listening post. In it, subtext could be explored (not that subtext was part of my vocabulary or understanding at the time). Endless questions asked. Links made. There was a saying, 'Actions speak louder than words.' I'd noticed a contradiction between actions and words. Why did I sometimes do the opposite of what I'd said I was going to do? And adults did it, too.

SU passages became less important. Private reading more so. Psalms read like riddles and were beautiful when chanted. Proverbs were said to be very wise. Miracles in the Gospel stories were awesome. Some of St Paul's letters to the Corinthians and Ephesians were inspired but St Paul always seemed very bossy, especially in regard to women, which indicated, to me, that he'd probably never had to help with the ironing.

Late teens. Bible study. I mention how difficult it is reading

Robert's (abridged) copy of *The Confessions of St Augustine*. There's an audible gasp.

The study leader is quick to tell me I'm straying in my reading. 'You only have to believe and study the Bible. Leave the rest to us.'

I was waiting on a missionary call, similar to the one Corrie Ten Boom received. She was a tiny dynamo of a woman, who spoke at our church when she was in the country. She said she received her calling as a mature-age woman. I wasn't that old, so it meant there was still hope.

Corrie's writings, especially *Amazing Love*, were highly influential. Her words set me on a personal quest for Holiness. Whatever was read back then moved and inspired. Those books were so inspiring I'd copy out passages into a notebook and dip into them later. I still keep notebooks of inspiration today.

Ten Boom and Amy Carmichael, another amazing missionary, were brave souls who helped shape my belief that, with prayer, even the impossible could be faced front-on. They helped clarify perspectives on life. Their tales interpreted events in a symbolic, poetic way. They looked for deeper patterns, spiritual patterns found in thought and patterns of behaviour.

When Ruby was asked for her opinion on these matters, she wasn't sure.

'But, Mum, you should know.' After all, she was almost equal to God.

There was a convent at nearby Naremburn on the same grounds of the primary school which Stanley and his siblings had attended. My father had cousins who were priests and nuns. Whenever he happened upon nuns, walking in pairs, on their way back to the convent, he'd always stop and offer them a lift. If the car was full, we'd just have to squish up.

I remember one very hot day Stanley saw two sisters walking back from a pastoral visit in searing heat, in heavy garb. I was surprised to feel the gruff texture of sister's black habit when she sat beside me.

While Stan chatted to these very reverent sisters, I stared at the stiff white strips of starch that plastered their foreheads. It also worried me that my father was joking with them. It seemed disrespectful, somehow. Yet, when the sisters alighted, they turned, blessed us and thanked Stanley. I felt so proud to think that someone like God knew my father's name.

Len, Stan, Robert, Ruby, Anne sitting on running board of 1928 Dodge.

Holidays at The Entrance. L to R: Robert, Len, Anne, Stan holding Wendy.

5
68 Penshurst Street

Out the back of 68, long before they pulled the old house down to build a service station, I had a garden. It was in the days before Italians arrived in Penshurst Street with their bright garden statues and colourful ornaments. Before the Italians, my garden was probably too ornate for Willoughby. It was bordered with small painted stones, high gloss yellow and black paint, leftovers, standard colours which Stan always used when repainting the kitchen.

A few years later, my pastel statues would've turned green with envy had they seen the glory of the small Italian gardens across the road, a few doors down, with their embroidered edges lining narrow side paths of semis.

These newcomers, from a far-away land, had statues that held their colour: bright red, emerald green, dense powder blue. People commented to one another that these gardens were 'too loud'. Secretly, I adored them.

My garden was decorated with plaster of Paris Humpty Dumpties, rabbits and lions. I'd buy sixpence-worth of plaster of Paris from the produce store a few doors down. The lady always scooped up the fine powder and filled the small brown paper bag till overflowing. She'd put it inside a bigger bag so it wouldn't spill on the way home, where I could hardly wait to mix it and pour into rubber moulds. Many a rabbit's ear broke off because the mould was peeled back too soon. Bright paint was thickly applied but the statues always dried pastel.

I'd always wanted a garden. No, I needed a garden. Discussions were held as to where. Half the backyard was already under cultivation.

Chook yards took up the back stretch. The middle strip was comprised of the essential cricket pitch, which was sacrosanct. It was swept every day because it was the main pathway to the chooks and it was also used for games like fly and hopscotch, provided the boys weren't using it. My garden was to be a narrow strip along the northern bathroom end of the house.

Stan dug it up and loosened the soil in the small patch, parallel to Gran's garden along the back veranda. Ruby donated a starter pack of seeds: cosmos and asters. Soon the youngest gardener was the proud owner of her own watering can.

It was exciting to pick flowers and mix them with Ruby's fresh delights from her front and side gardens. The joy of gardening fed an innate love of line, texture, colour. It was a happy place. There were new green shoots and starbursts of colour.

At one end of the garden, an asparagus fern stitched itself to the southern side of the fence. The fern, with its hidden bite, wove its chartreuse threads in and around the palings. It complemented the yellow, red, pink and mauve surprises popping up in my garden. It was the place to sit and soak up solitude like a happy frog in water.

Fairies lived in dewdrops hanging on delicate asparagus fern. Many of them flew around in the filtered light. My breath was the wind and I blew them gently, higher and higher and then they'd float slowly back down. Mummy said fairies didn't like being disturbed because they were so busy; especially tooth fairies.

My garden had boundaries and so did I. Clear, simple boundaries. I knew where I was, who I was. Family. A gardener like my father, mother and great-grandmother.

Stan's potato patch was full of hidden treasures. He dug trenches around it and wired it with scallops of hope. Ruby's garden was the cottage potpourri out the front. She also tended to the side passage which lit up with hydrangeas, snowdrops, jonquils and freesias.

Gran's garden thrived outside the back door. Its boundaries were less noticeable when compared with the deep trenches around Stan's potato patch. Her garden was laden with peas, beans, carrots, celery, onions, shallots, rhubarb. The pumpkin vine ran freely around the yard. It liked to climb the old rooster fence alongside the indestructible choko vine.

Before Ruby set to work each day, she was in the habit of picking a young carrot and cutting it into rings. She'd store it in her apron pocket to nibble on while she worked. Unfortunately for Peta Rabbit, she had to change her addictive, nibbling ways when her pigment turned yellow.

An extension to our backyard was a spare block of land behind our place. George, the fruiterer, leased it from the Hugheses, our next-door neighbours, who owned both back blocks.

George grew dahlias there and sold them at markets. At certain times of the year, they were a shimmering palette and their glamorous heads turned towards the light. When sitting on an overhanging branch in the old mulberry tree up the back, a favoured position when seeking solitude, there were times when the thick, caramel hum of bees sounded and felt like Nature's pulse.

George stopped growing dahlias. We children held a strong belief that it was all because of Blackbeard. He lived in the back street, next to the spare block behind our place. He had no garden but high bushes which grew behind his fences. He had a hook for a hand and used to yell and throw bottles if we laughed or played too loud when building cubby houses out of George's left over wooden boxes. If anyone dared look up, Blackbeard's face would be there, pressed against the window. When he was angry, he'd bang on the side window with his hook and we'd dutifully scatter.

Blackbeard was the real bogeyman. Stan and Ruby insisted he had a mother who lived with him but bogeymen didn't have mothers. They weren't born. They just were. Although children were terrified of Blackbeard, Stan and Ruby always spoke kindly. 'Poor bugger,' Stan would say. 'Never came back the same.'

Our northern neighbours, the Hugheses, were a significant part of our protective world and, like our climbing rose, I too liked to head north, through the fence where two or three palings had been joined together to make a gate. All we had to do was remember to put the gate back. If we forgot to put it back, then Prince, our rather well-fed-nip-at-your-heels-if-I-don't-like-you cocker spaniel would follow.

In the right-hand back corner of the Hugheses' yard was a big shed with a mezzanine floor. A narrow cement path separated garden beds. The spare block of land behind their place announced every season. It had macadamias, grapevines, peach trees. More importantly, it gave us access to Ward Street with its manicured lawns and floral borders trimming cement driveways. Grassy nature strips carpeted well-established camphor laurels which stood patiently waiting for generations to climb into their welcoming arms.

One day, I climbed higher than usual and couldn't believe what I saw. A plan; a pattern laid out before me. Patterns were in every direction: roads, fences, footpaths, gutters, nature strips, poles, wires; all lines of direction. They weren't just wandering anywhere. They looked like they were all going somewhere. This amazing sight raised questions. Who made the plan? Why did our road go where it did? Why did it veer left at Laurel Street and not right? Who said? Why wasn't there a corner at our place? Why further down? Why was Penshurst Street a main road and not Ward Street? Who said so? And, why was it called Penshurst Street? Why was our street flat and then hilly?

Stan explained how we lived on a ridge and the roads followed old wallaby tracks. 'Aboriginal people would've followed them.'

'Does that mean there are wallabies in Willoughby? Are there? Where are they?'

'Well, Twerpo, over time things change –'

'Stan, don't start or there'll be no end to it.'

Things changed only after my fifth grade teacher told Mrs Butt that her daughter's continual asking of questions was not attention-seeking. The conscientious, overworked, exhausted mother seemed to accept the questioning, which often took up valuable time and energy which she really didn't have.

Robert, Len, Wendy and Anne.

*

'He who has a why to live for can bear almost any how.'
Friedrich Nietzsche

6
The Arts

Mrs Hughes regularly sat at her treadle sewing machine in their closed-in veranda. I'd stand beside her and watch. Her machine was more modern than ours. Our Singer sewing machine only had a handle. What was she doing? Why? How? She'd explain over the top of the regular pad-pad-pad-pad of the treadle.

We were allowed to play inside at the Hugheses', something we were never allowed to do at home, except for rainy days: then we could play on the back veranda. When inside, the Hugheses' had an attic room at the top of very steep stairs. Clifford and I often played with a model train set laid out on the attic floor. Clifford, the eldest of the four boys, and my very good friend, liked to make complicated adjustments to layouts. They always worked – that is, until one of the younger ones came in and started making their own adjustments.

Whenever Mrs H started to play the piano downstairs, I'd quietly slip away from the others and stand at the living room door and listen. Invariably, Mrs H saw me and would call me in and indicate to sit down, usually in the big armchair beside the china cabinet, which was full of fine porcelain and figurines.

She'd be rehearsing Sunday school choruses and hymns for the following Sunday morning at North Sydney Baptist Church.

After she finished and packed the chorus books into a folder, she'd play extemporaneously. That's when her whole body changed. She'd start to sway. Her forearms and wrists and fingers all became part of a gentle wave. The beauty of the music intoxicated the room. Even the fragrance from the roses, arranged in a small round vase on the side table, seemed to fill the air. Mrs H was centre stage and I was dress circle, speechless, weighed down by inexpressible beauty and blessedness.

'Joy, joy, joy, with joy my heart is ringing…'

Listening to the mini-recitals created an ache to learn the piano. It was the same ache when thinking about ballet. Mrs H offered to teach me piano but Mrs Butt felt it would be intruding. Mrs H offered the use of her piano for practice.

On my birthday, I received a children's mini portable white grand piano. It had pride of place for a while at one end of the dining room table. White notes played. Black notes were painted on for effect. There was a music book with popular children's songs like 'Twinkle, Twinkle, Little Star'. My friend who had real piano lessons taught me simple scales. She was very strict and freely hit me over the knuckles with a ruler if I made a mistake; a giggling matter between friends. Years later, I returned the compliment when helping her with maths.

At the far end of the Hugheses' big double room was the dining room with tall bookcases. An audible hush threw its cloak over the room. It felt like a hush that seemed to belong to the knowledge in the big, leather bound encyclopaedias. I liked to sit and look at them and knew that one day I'd have big bookcases, just like these, and I'd fill them with important books. The Hugheses' was my spiritual home away from home.

The Webster's Dictionary was first sighted by my parents at the Hordern Pavilion at Sydney Royal Easter Show at Moore Park. Uncle Will, my mother's uncle, was manager of the Pavilion and we'd meet up each year with extended family, gathering in his small office. As more family congregated, we'd spill out into the staff tea room.

Webster's New Twentieth Century Dictionary of the English Language, Unabridged (1952), linen-bound, cost five pounds. Stan and Ruby put it on lay-by and paid it off in instalments.

They were feeling embarrassed that their eldest son, Robert, had missed out on a place at Artarmon Opportunity School for Fifth and Sixth Grades because, as the headmaster explained, while he was eligible, they noted he didn't have access to a set of encyclopaedias in the home for private study. Little did they know about Stan and Ruby's tight budgeting and savings routine. They would've made it possible to buy a set, even if it meant Stan mowed an extra lawn in his lunch hour or Ruby made an extra couple of dozen string bags for the small company which paid her sweatshop rates. But, in time, it was a fortuitous decision for the gifted young athlete because his lifetime focus would be sport.

When the *Webster's* arrived at 68, it was given pride of place at the end of our very large mahogany dining table, the same table which Stan's family had gathered around when he was a boy.

Its first page, '*Webster's*…based upon the broad foundations laid down by Noah Webster, Revised by…' was solemnly read by Stan, while we crowded around. We looked in awe at the few coloured pages. We marvelled at the sight of three thousand black and white illustrations and the detailed maps at the back. This was going to be an invaluable resource for school projects. It smelt heavenly and really needed its own lectern. I could see it resting on the back of a highly polished brass eagle just like the one at church which held the Holy Bible. And there was a link. An important one.

John 1:1 'In the beginning was the Word and the Word was with God, and the Word was God…'.

The Webster's Dictionary was important, like a sacred place for Stan, who sat there, night after night, poring over its revelations. He'd find some fantastical new word: 'Get a load of this.'

He helped us understand pronunciation and enunciation symbols. It was fun. We'd laugh at our strangulated attempts and Stan would put new words into a comedic context. The easiest way to learn was always with laughter.

Standing beside my father as if exploring chapter and verse, it felt like I was standing in a sacred place, like in church, listening to the Gospel being read.

It was clear that I was a reader like my father, paternal grandmother and maternal great-grandmother: I was Katy in *What Katy Did at School*, a mixture of Enid Blyton's characters in the Famous Five, and had a definite affinity with Anne in *Anne of Green Gables*. At Sunday school, I was Pilgrim in *Pilgrim's Progress* and tried to identify with the most excellent Mary in *Mary Jones and her Bible* but whenever Mary suffered an injustice she never complained. It was beyond my comprehension. Why couldn't she speak up about the unfairness, the injustice? I tried to live by her standards but couldn't.

My sixth grade teacher encouraged me to enter an art competition. I sat on the back veranda step and chose Prince, our fat, black cocker spaniel as subject. He didn't realise he was posing. The form didn't seem quite right but Ruby said there was a likeness.

Embarrassed when handing in the painting, I was later surprised to learn from the teacher that Prince been chosen to be exhibited in David Jones's city store, in an exhibition showing the diversity of children's art in primary schools. The budding artist skipped all the way home, in disbelief, wanting to share her joy with the whole world.

Did we see the exhibition? I can't remember. There's a hint of a memory but based on what Ruby believed about such matters, the memory could be more to do with my imagination. It was always best to keep achievements quiet otherwise it could be considered showing off or, worse still, it might make siblings feel left out. Mrs H was told. I knew she wouldn't tell anyone.

Stan said in a quiet aside, 'Good on you, Twerpo.'

The Webster's Dictionary was also a source of inspiration for illustration imitation. Empty jam tins were another source. The tins were soaked until the shiny wrappings peeled off and were dried flat on a tea towel. Pictures of blackberries, peaches, apricots were cut out. Their fruit, leaves, blossoms were pasted into an old scrapbook; a fine introduction to still life.

In high school, my art teacher, Mrs S, selected a graphite sketch to go to China to be hung in an international exhibition of students' work. The drawing was of an old Federation house on the other side of the road, opposite the school. The drawing could not be returned. No problem. Being chosen was reward enough.

Drawing added meaning: the silent, split-second sightings of rainbows on oily wet roads, buds opening, the new green shoot, the irregular outline of houses against the light sky; all essential dreaming; soul seeds being sown for a later harvest.

Family holidays. Back row L to R: Ern, Stan, Nell, Gell, Ruby. Front row L to R: Dennis, Anne, Wendy, Grahame.

7
Kings and Queens

School holidays were always busy. Rugs needed to be spread out under the shade of the old pepper tree. No sooner would rugs be spread than they'd be filled with small children. Funny stories were made up about them, which always caught their attention. Sometimes, we cut out pictures from magazines and pasted them onto butcher's paper with lumpy glue made out of plain flour and water.

Another holiday activity was for the younger children to sit in rows on the toilet steps. We'd fill up any spare places with teddy bears and dolls. I'd make up plays; write up everyone's idea for a play on the back veranda wall with chalk. We'd work out who wanted to be what. Later ,the play, with all the desired characters – kings, queens, princesses – would be written in quiet time after actors went home. There'd be copies made for each one, with their part underlined.

It was important that everyone had lines, both to keep their attention and to be fair. This meant that, by necessity, the storyline was wildly contorted. Similar techniques would be used some forty years later with my daughter and her friends. They wanted a play with a dragon, princess, knights, a king and queen and, of course, it had to be funny. *Royal Tears* was the result, a play written for primary school children, published on two occasions by the NSW Department of Education's *School Magazine*. In essence, there was very little difference in the process between my writing of *Royal Tears* and the plays written when sitting on the back steps at 68.

Often, actors grew restless and wandered off, bored with waiting in the wings. That taught me a valuable lesson: not to be precious about my work. It was a miracle if surviving fragments of script made it back to the next rehearsal. Some plays came to fruition. World premières were held in our backyards. Kitchen chairs were carried out, enough to cater for the audience, our parents. The stage would be set by turning the rickety old birdcage upside down. It was risky standing on rotting wood. The main stage was in front, on the ground. Parents and neighbours donated bottles of lemonade and iced patty cakes. There was a small entry fee. Lolly wages.

Sometimes, an actor giggled when they shouldn't and this made the audience giggle. Being a conscientious producer and director, my concern was that, because of the unexpected ripples of laughter coming from the audience, they might miss important lines. Some had covered their faces with their hands. Some were doubled up as if with stomach cramp. But, in spite of these hiccups, there was always enthusiastic whistling, loud applause and cheers. And our shows went on and on.

At times, our backyard was miraculously empty. This meant I could lie down under the old pepper or peach tree, without interruption, and wonder why we lived in this house. Why this street? This suburb? Could you live up there in the sky? Walk on the clouds? Soon, my brothers would find me lying under one of the trees near where they played cricket. They'd be batsmen and bowler. I was allowed to be fielder or wicketkeeper. The Ashes were only ever played with a well polished six-stitcher. If the batsmen missed the ball and the ball missed the stumps, it most certainly never missed my nose or fumbling fingers.

I'd complain. 'I want to bat' or 'I want to bowl.'

'You can't bowl underarm in cricket.'

If the reluctant fielder was given a turn, the batsman and bowler knew it'd only be for a ball or two. My personal preference was to be in a left-right-out prone position under the shadiest tree. And, today, with the ultraviolet scare, it never ceases to amaze me that cricket grounds don't provide shady trees for fielders at a sensible distance from the pitch.

During one of those rare moments of solitude, lying under the middle-aged apple tree, next to the chooks, I noticed the moon was out. How could that be? It shouldn't be there, should it? It's daytime. Something's wrong. I want to race inside to tell my mother but can't move. Grip the lowest branch closest to me because there's a strong tug between the moon and me. Somehow, it's lulling. Do we belong? Are we connected? If so, is it me to it or it to me?

I ran inside. 'Mum, the moon's out. It shouldn't be. It's not night.'
'That happens sometimes.'
'Why?'
'Ask your father when he gets home. I haven't got time right now.'

Another favourite tree in the backyard is an ancient peach. It's in full bloom. I lie under it on the plush, cool grass. I spread my arms to mirror the spreading branches. There's an inner-under beauty; quiet, church-like, great bone-dome lines where sometimes pigeons, sparrows and magpies swoop. Light shines through the canopy revealing the underside of leaves.

I become aware of transparency, although I don't know its name. The midday sun filters through the filigreed spread, revealing hidden veins. Are they the same for each leaf? If so, who organised it? Does anyone else know about it? If so, why aren't we talking about it?

I pluck a leaf. Hold it in my palm. Nothing much to see. When I hold it up to the light again, there are the glorious intricate pathways. I'm part of this light and shade and can feel light shining on me. Is it shining through me like it shines through the leaves?

The peach tree and I spread against the blue of the sky. Light and I are part of it. That's when there's the realisation that the sky is right down beside me. Put out my hands and try to hold pieces of sky but can't seem to grasp any. I'm aware of feeling light, lighter than the leaves; lighter than light. Am afraid. Grip the grass with one hand and a branch with the other. Feel light enough to float up off into the sky and no one will know where I am.

I try standing but legs are too heavy. Shaking, stumbling as I run, trying to outrun fear, I head towards the safety of the back veranda, lugging the enormity of the experience with me. Stand close beside my mother, who prepares vegies for dinner. Heart stops racing. Want to ask my mother what happened but can't put it into words.

Ruby picked fresh vegies out of the garden as often as she could. One day, when too young to know any better, I picked some beans out of Gran's garden, just like Gran picked them. Chopped them up. As a surprise, I decided to be Mother and cook tea for the family on the gas stove. Lit the gas with the gas gun and put my plastic toy saucepan on the flame. Soon there was a rush of black smoke and molten plastic dripping everywhere. What was happening?

Suddenly, Mummy was there. She turned off the gas at the main, all the while explaining that my saucepans couldn't be used for cooking on a real stove. Absolutely appalled. Did this mean that this cooking set couldn't be used? What a lie of a toy! It was immediately relegated for use in the garden, where we were always making and baking mushy, mud pies in the sun oven outside.

Royal Tears.

8
New Neighbours

New neighbours arrived on the southern side of 68 Penshurst Street. The once under-inhabited, three-bedroom brick bungalow was too small for the new family. Their father worked long hours, sometimes seven days a week. The youngest slept in a drawer on the floor. It was hard not to look at them as we walked past; naked children sitting on the front steps crying. Sometimes, we'd hear their mother crying in the front bedroom.

Snot hung from toddlers' nostrils. It sucked in and out with each sob; repulsive but fascinating to watch. Sometimes dry, crackled snot smeared their white cheeks. They never used hankies. Hankies at our place always smelt like Persil. They were crisp, ironed, no creases in the corner. They were ironed into a triangle.

We always carried a hanky. At infants' school, a clean hankie had to be pinned to our tunic every day. We'd be inspected every morning at assembly. If you didn't have a clean handkerchief, you had to stand out the front and be shamed.

At home, if there were tears, Ruby would pull out a handkerchief that smelt like apple blossom. She'd pat-pat our nose and dry our cheeks then tell us to be on our way.

If Stan was there, he'd pull out a man-sized hanky which was kept in his side trouser pocket and always felt warm and smelt of Ruby Red tobacco. He'd shake the hanky with a flourish and hold it to the nose and say, 'A good blow. Hard, harder.' Then he'd look at the crumpled hankie and complain. 'Look what you've done. You've blown a hole in the wretched thing.'

Laughter would mix with tears. But life wasn't like that for the children next door.

Mrs Butt and Mrs Hughes befriended the young, sensitive mother of five and soon they there were sharing morning teas and gentle hints about cooking and housekeeping. The older girls were given ironing lessons by Mrs Butt, which, to my amazement, the girls enjoyed. Their mother was taught practical short cuts to housekeeping and how to set up a routine and how to discipline her lovely, lively children. And, importantly, they encouraged her to take time out of each day to do something for herself. 'Do something you love.' They were speaking from experience. Mrs Hughes loved playing the piano and sewing and Mrs Butt loved knitting intricate patterns and gardening.

The artist painted life-size Disney characters on her children's bedroom walls. Soon we were wishing we had bedrooms like theirs. She started a major project: an original frieze which ran all along the sides of the hallway and right the way around their crowded living room. It was as if the grapevine grew while everyone was asleep, which was partly true because often the only time the young mother could paint was when the children were asleep.

Eventually the not-so-new children were allowed to climb through fences on one condition: that when necessary they use the toilet and not the backyard. They also had to wash their hands afterwards. This was a delightful novelty for them: clean hands, pink cheeks and clean clothes, and hankies that mostly stayed in their pockets.

9

Keeper of the Watch

Reading nurtured my limited awareness of how, why, when and where. Parents knew everything but there came a time when books, magazines and newspapers became an additional source. Because it was in print, I assumed every word was true.

There were many articles and pictures in the newspaper about new German planes. Germans had something to do with the war and dropping bombs in England. It was important to watch out for every plane. Best to check them.

Even Gran said when she looked at a plane flying overhead, 'You'll never get me up in one of those.' She must've said that because she knew it was mainly Germans who flew them.

When six or seven years of age, there was a headline on page three or four of the *Daily Mirror*, or was it the *Telegraph*? It read, 'Third World War.' Unable to read the full article, the young reader was alarmed. Stan read the newspaper every night but he didn't seem at all upset at about the threat of another war.

If there was worry in the house, it usually moved in whispers or dim murmurings, after lights out, in Stan and Ruby's bedroom. But there were no whisperings, no murmurings. Daddy must've missed the page about the war.

Next night.

'Daddy, it says in the paper there's going to be a war.'

'No chance, Twerpo.'

'It's in the paper.'

Gran said, 'I told you she's too young to be reading that thing.'

Stan said, 'Here, give me a look.'

But the headline was in the previous day's paper, which had already been used to help light the fire under the copper which heated the water for our afternoon baths.

Uncle Bill, who sat at one end of the table, with Burma Road horrors still in his bones, chipped in. 'If there is one, I hope it's bloody well over before we know it. Booom.'

Why weren't my parents concerned about the Germans and their new planes? The planes could fly over any night now when we were asleep and booooom. It was said we lived on a flight path. If that was the case then there was good reason to worry about the sound of every plane when lying in bed. It could mean only one thing. The Germans were turning the flight path into a road wide enough for bombers. The Germans were clever. Everyone said so.

World War II continued in our house long after the war finished. A long line of family soldiers' portraits remained a fixture on our living room picture railings for years to come. Fortunately, only one uncle was killed in action. The other two were missing in action: prisoners of war at Changi and Japanese camps. Thankfully, both survived but it was everyone's war and my war, too. At night, many a battlefield was visited. The faces on the wall played their part.

It's the middle of the night. Heart pounding in time with soldiers' feet, marching, marching up the street: left, right, left, right. I creep over to the window. If soldiers try to climb through our window, we can hide under the beds or in the wardrobe.

Head down. Listening. Soldiers marching? Nothing. Quiet. Kneeling on polished floorboards hurts bare knees. No soldiers. Not yet. Must've gone up Mowbray Road. Back into bed with blankets pulled up. Like Uncle Bill said, 'They'll come at night and boom. We won't know anything about it.'

For the next day or so, newspapers are scoured but nothing more is written about a Third World War. The fearful battle of the night fades like portraits on the wall.

*

Yesterday is gone and its tale told.
Today new seeds are growing.

Rumi

Gran and Ruby.

68 Penshurst Street: Len, Anne, Wendy, Robert.

10

Margot Fonteyn

Out the front of 68, long before they pulled down the old Scout hall which stood directly across the road, I learnt ballet. Every Saturday morning, it was time to drape myself over the front fence and watch girls arrive in a frothy swirl of twirling tights and tutus. Even though some of the girls were from school, it was accepted practice not to wave to one another on Saturday mornings because across the road was a whole world away.

Pretend ballet slippers curled between the fading front pickets and, as I leant forward, it was easy to see the ballet teacher walk around the corner before the others saw her. Whenever the ballet girls caught sight of their teacher, they'd squeal and race to meet her. Whoever reached first would hold her hand all the way back to the Scout hall. The teacher would unlock the heavy wooden doors and hold one of them open and say, 'In we go.' Sometimes she'd glance across and smile. Not everyone recognised the ballerina in me.

Ruby thought the teacher 'very big'. Gran agreed. She thought she was 'a bit of a hussy…bottle blonde…that ponytail…red fingernails. No daughter of mine would…' And she was right. The teacher didn't look anything like Margot Fonteyn, my idol, who danced in the *Women's Weekly* cut-outs sticky-taped to the back of my bedroom door.

My ballet slippers were actually black physical culture slippers worn every Monday night at Girls' Club. There was a spare card of black bias binding and large safety pins in the sewing basket. On a Saturday morning, bias binding would be pinned to the slippers and tied in the same way satin ribbons were tied on the ballet slippers by the ballerinas across the road. The criss-cross of laces flattered band-aided legs. The black laces transformed into pink ones. They looked classical. All five feet positions were religiously practised along with casual tutoring by ballet friends and hints taken from storybooks and I always practised under the watchful eye of Margot.

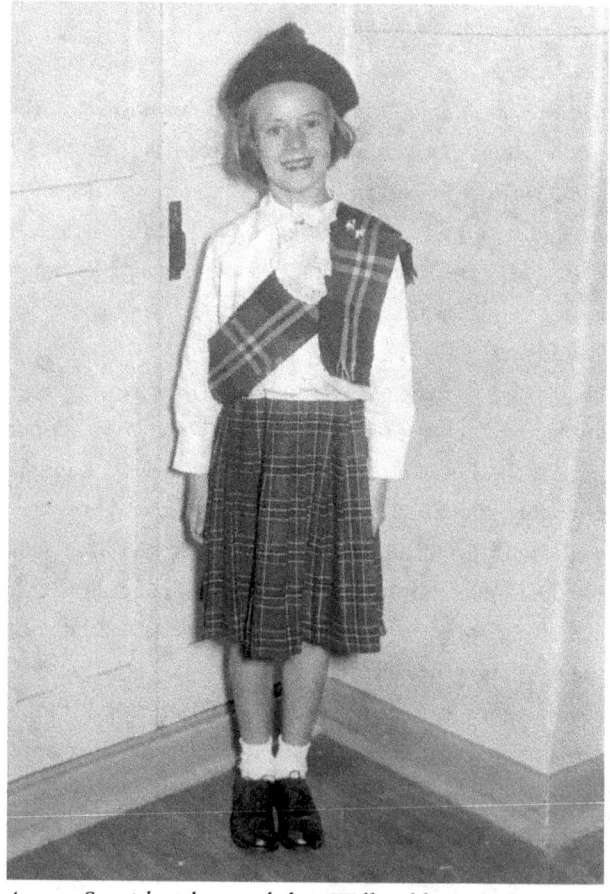

Anne – Scottish girl, second class, Willoughby Primary concert.

11
A Beloved Room-mate

Gran was a strong character and every bit as determined as our family doctor. Dr W was a giant of a man in both stature and spirit. When he visited Gran, there were often loud arguments. One time, he organised an enema for her but she was adamant.

'Don't waste your time. I'm not having it.'

Dr W said if she refused to cooperate with the nurse, he'd do it himself. 'You're a stubborn old mule,' and he left the room laughing.

'You needn't bother calling again on my account.'

On the Day of the Enema, Ruby was tense. It was school holidays and we were all home. It looked like they were preparing for Gran to die, because I'd overheard aunties and uncles say how cruel it was to give Mother an enema. 'It'll be too much for her, Ruby. It's on your head.'

We were ushered out the back and told not to come near the house until further notice. The copper was filled with water and the fire lit. It was a long morning in the backyard. Had the nurse arrived? While we played, my ears were finely tuned to any sound of agony coming from inside. Enemas must be really serious because Ruby refused to explain the ins and outs. 'It's not something you talk about.' So it was left to my imagination.

It's quiet. Gran must've died. They're probably kneeling beside her bed, heads bowed, sobbing. A loud cheer? Cheering? Laughing? Clapping? They're clapping?

Gran's spine finally gave way when she was eighty-seven, requiring full-time care. She was so sick with pneumonia it was said she wouldn't last the week. During that time, after school, we took turns at sitting by her side. We'd crinkle Gran's paper-thin skin, squeezing it gently, leaving fine dehydrated pin tucks all the way down her arm. We'd count how long it took for them to disappear.

Ruby would come into the bedroom from time to time. She'd sponge Gran's forehead with a mixture of warm water and vinegar; a smell that would make anyone sick. At times, Gran was delirious. She'd hallucinate, which was disturbing.

Ruby would come in and check. 'Are you all right?'

'She's been telling me about a beautiful white horse. She said it's up over there on the ridge. A man's riding it. She says it's George.'

Before Gran was so sick and dependent, a miracle had occurred at Penshurst Street over the years. Stan and Gran had become best friends. In her final years at 68, she would only allow Stanley to carry her from the bed to her cane chair so she could sit in the sun outside.

Eventually, Stan and Ruby's efforts to keep her at home were not enough. Two people were needed to hold her in place on the bedpan. It was time for Gran to go into a nursing home where staff could look after her. Another onset of pneumonia settled the issue.

The day she was moved into a convalescent home in Chatswood, not expected to live more than a week, everyone hovered slipper-quiet.

When I bent over to kiss my room-mate, she looked quite scared. They carried her out on the stretcher.

'Out of the way,' she said. 'Let the young men through.'

The ambulance men, who looked old, carried her frail body on the stretcher out the front and down the steps, and Gran could be heard talking, in good cheer, as if she was lightening their load. 'There's a first for everything…never been to hospital…had all my children at home.'

There was a radical change without Gran in the house. The boys turned up the radio, somersaulted over lounges, did backflips along the hall, handstands against the wall. There didn't seem to be enough room anywhere.

The bedroom was a good place to sit and cry. When would my beloved room-mate come home? I fretted at the sight of her empty bed. Couldn't watch her read any more. No glass of water sitting there, soaking teeth that used to smile at me. No more watching her hunt down imaginary fleas between the sheets in her bed; a hangover, Ruby said, from the days when she took sick animals to bed

We weren't allowed in our bedrooms unless it was bedtime but I used to slip in anyway and hope my mother didn't know.

'Stay out here with the rest of us, please.'

'It's too noisy.'

'They're just boys being boys.'

'It's too noisy.'

'You'll get used to it.'

But no. And when we visited Gran at the convalescent home, we never got used to seeing her cry. During the visits, she'd beg Stan and Ruby to take her home. After the visit, we'd climb into the car and Ruby would sit there and wipe her eyes.

'I feel so guilty. If only her back was stronger.'

Stan would blow his nose. 'Poor bugger.'

One night, when we were about to leave, Gran wouldn't let go of my hand.

My parents said, 'Come on,' and they walked out the door, but it was hard to pull away.

'You've got to get me out of here. I have to come home. You tell them.' She let me go with a promise.

Childlike skills of persuasion and negotiation were ineffective. Afterwards, there was news that Gran would never be coming home again. My promise had been broken. Utterly inconsolable. You can't break promises.

Miraculously, Gran passed the three weeks' crisis and was moved into more permanent accommodation: a family run nursing home at Five Dock, close to where her eldest daughter lived. Gran lay there, bedridden, for eight years, as alert as any member of staff, all of whom treated her with great respect. Often she was the only one in her section whose brain fully functioned, so the staff would come in and talk to her.

The nursing home was a large two-storey Victorian home with generous windows and French doors which opened onto sun-drenched verandas. Beds were tucked into nooks and crannies so it felt more like a family home than a ward.

Gran's family worked out a roster so she had someone visit her almost every day. She soon became aware of the needs of those around her so, by the time we arrived for our weekly visits, she would've worked out a roster for us – whom we should visit.

'Go and see Mrs H. She hasn't had a visitor all week. And Mrs So and So. She's looking forward to seeing you.'

So my sister and I would go and talk to the ladies in the ward. Some would remember us. We'd listen to their stories, often the same story, again and again.

Over the years, Stan and Ruby received many urgent calls to come in when it was thought Gran was 'on her last'.

The phone at 68 Penshurst Street never stopped ringing. We shared a party line and the other party was not impressed by its increased use. Ruby felt pressured and was always apologising to the other party. Neighbourly relations were good but both families were relieved when they got their own line.

Relatives who visited Gran in the nursing home would ring Ruby with advice and with endless helpful suggestions concerning Mother's care. One of my jobs was to take messages; an apprentice diplomat, indirectly involved in family politics; a deflecting screen for Ruby from more difficult family members. 'If X asks if Y has rung, say you don't know, which you don't.' Understood.

It was also more obvious now why my parents were so tired. While it seemed it'd be easier having Gran in a nursing home – that is, not having to care for her 24/7 and not having to cook for and feed the constant stream of visitors – it was, in another way, just as hard. In the late 1950s, both Stan and Ruby suffered from nervous exhaustion and several nervous collapses.

Six months after Nanna died, our dear Gran died, aged ninety-five, in May 1962. I was still considered too young to go to her funeral but was old enough to know that, for Gran, dying was a blessed relief.

While Gran lived with us, the radio volume was always kept low to moderate but after Gran moved out, there was a strong 2CH influence throughout the house, except in the early mornings, when Ruby preferred 2UE.

She used the radio as an alarm clock. 'Wakey, wakey, rise and shine,' she'd say when she came bounding into our bedrooms. She sounded like the most annoying, chirpiest budgerigar on the block, even surpassing the crazed, fictional Sammy the Sparrow on 2UE.

The radio volume was only ever turned up after Ruby finished her Quiet Time. She'd sit and knit intricate patterns for an hour or so of a morning after Stan left for work and before any of our toes touched the ground.

Seven o'clock. Volume up. *Top Forty Pops* raging down the hallway and into every room.

Head sheltering under the blanket, I'd beg, 'Please turn the radio down.' For me, the only way to tune into a day was a decibel at a time.

'Not until you're up and moving.'

Stumbling out, eyes half-open, desperate fingers search for the volume knob.

*

'Quiet is turning down the volume knob on life.'

Khaled Hosseini

12

A Social Embarrassment

I always felt awkward with my developing body and it became increasingly important to be well covered at all times. If not, it was said, it could draw unwelcome attention. The attentions had something to do with men. Some men, it seemed, were easily swayed and you had to watch out for yourself because, at times, some of them, not all, could be a nuisance and for this reason it was advisable never to draw attention to yourself. Lipstick, small heels and shaved legs were out of the question until mid-teens.

It was only after my brother Len convinced our mother that his sister was a social embarrassment to him that I was allowed to wear the palest pink lipstick. He also offered to buy me a pair of black ,low-heeled, patent leather court shoes. His sister, he said, was dressed too much like a square, nothing like his widgie girlfriends. 'And she should be shaving her legs. They're too hairy. That's what girls do.'

Ruby had almost hair-free legs while mine, left unchecked, could keep me warm in winter. It'd be a couple more years before my friend's oldest sister, who was a nurse, conducted a Hairy Leg Rescue Mission. Ruby was horrified. How dare they! She couldn't believe that someone outside the family would take it upon themselves to override her wishes. But they understood. With hairy legs, it was so uncomfortable wearing thick winter school stockings. Even so, Ruby remained indignant.

My brothers often talked in hushed tones about the girls they'd taken out the night before. Big Ears grew wary, never wanting to be discussed and rated as a product in the way the boys described their dates.

Ruby disapproved of her sons' talk. 'I hope you always show them respect. Treat them as if they were your sister.'

Loud laughter. 'If they were anything like my sister, I wouldn't be taking them out.'

'You know what I mean. I want no son of mine getting any girl into trouble. It's a terrible thing for the girl and the baby. It's up to you.'

My brothers had to be careful with girls and I had to be careful with boys.

'And remember, sit like a young lady, not like you're in jeans, and don't go looking at or smiling at boys. They might get the wrong idea and don't flirt. Nice girls don't flirt.'

Apparently flirts were 'common'. They smiled at men and 'went all the way'. What did 'all the way' mean? It seemed to have something to do with 'never the same'.

Menstruation was my next stumbling block. It was solely responsible for being no longer allowed to wear my favourite green jeans.

'And no more lying on the floor.'

'But I love lying on the floor.'

'Get up and sit on that chair properly. You're a young lady now.'

Even after the Mother and Daughter film night, there was confusion. Sex education. Hens, eggs, roosters, tadpoles on the screen. They had something to do with puberty.

Puberty was one of those whispered words among women. 'She's going through puberty.' How did they know? Where did you have to go to go through it? How long did it take? How many times did you have to go through it? What did it have to do with chooks and roosters?

To my astonishment, at film night, we were told we'd soon be producing eggs. Not eggs like the ones on the screen: the eggs in question had something to do with the illustration on screen. Arrows pointed between a naked man and woman who stood side by side. Arrows? Going between men and women? I'd never seen arrows like that, ever. How, when did they start? After the arrows came tadpoles, eggs, babies. Then there was more talk about eggs and blood. Blood?

Walking home in the dark, arm in arm with my mother, it felt we were starting out on a mysterious journey into a whole new world.

'Menst-r-u-a-tion? How will I know?'

'There'll be a spot of blood…come and tell me when it happens. That's all you need to know for now.'

Tall for my age and thin, in sixth class, with breasts mere buttons compared to some of my peers, Lennie, who was in second year high school, was annoyingly interested in them. One day as he walked past in the hallway, he teased again. I was very self-conscious of them at that stage. I hunched my shoulders to hide the mystery that was taking place.

Lennie asked for the thousandth time if he could see them. 'What do they look like?'

'I'm sick of this,' and pulled up my top. 'Look. See. Nothing to see,' then pulled the top down.

'Yes, there is. Can I touch them?'

'No. Go away.'

'Mum,' Len shouted, 'Anne showed her titties.'

Ruby hurried in. 'You what?'

'He's driving me mad. He's always teasing, wanting to see them. I want to shut him up.'

'You showed me your titties.' The inquisitor was in shock. He looked to his mother.

Ruby frowned. 'Don't do that again. And as for you, young man, leave her alone, once and for all.'

And he did.

Menstruation started well before some of my more buxom friends. It didn't seem right. Large-breasted girls always appeared more mature. They were showered with attention and favour from fashion and boys, boys, boys. There was often discreet discussion at our all girls' school about improving one's breast size. One buxom friend told us less buxom ones that if we pulled our breasts very hard, day and night, they'd grow to the desired size. It was such a boring task I didn't persist.

13

Cremorne Girls High

My former fifth grade teacher, Mrs L, lived down the road. She stopped me in the street one afternoon. She'd heard that my high school application form hadn't been received.

How to tell Mrs L about the negative effect my unpopular personal choice of high school was having at home, without seeming to blame my parents for the delay, was difficult. Nor could she be told about the whispered talk that took place at the kitchen table of an evening between them. It was always just out of earshot but it had something to do with the application form.

The delay to answer prompted Mrs L to ask, 'Is there a problem?'

There was a problem. Ruby wanted me to change my high school preferences before Stan signed. But it was impossible because I had a drive within me, which said you're going to Cremorne. It was a knowing. 'Mum wants me to go to Willoughby because it's across the road and they have second-hand uniforms.'

It was an important day when representatives from the three high schools addressed a special assembly for year six. Each speaker explained why their high school would be best for us and they told us what they had to offer. Two schools, Cremorne Girls and North Sydney Girls, were selective, so if we applied for them it didn't mean we'd be successful.

One of the speakers said that Cremorne Girls High was particularly interested in the Arts. They had extracurricular activities: visits from members of the Australian Ballet and the budding Opera Australia and visits to the Sydney Symphony in the Town Hall.

Arts were my daydream world. My best friend and my keen, performing self would improvise in her downstairs rumpus room before an appreciative, imaginary audience. As Margot, we'd perform *Swan Lake*. Sometimes we conducted the Sydney Symphony Orchestra. We sang, as we did in the combined school choir in the Sydney Town Hall with music maestro, Terrance Hunt. There was no question which school would be the most suitable.

'Tell your mother I said most schools have second-hand uniforms. And tell her I said Cremorne would be good for you and if she has any questions to please ask.'

Could've kissed Mrs L's feet. Thank you, thank you. Raced home. The deal was sealed. They'd take notice of a teacher.

'What were you doing telling her our…? She's not the one who… It's all right for her… I'll talk to your father tonight.'

That night, Stan signed the form. I'm assuming fingers were crossed that I wouldn't get in and would attend Willoughby Girls, which was directly across the road.

Mrs L sealed my high school fate that day.

After I was accepted, it was soon clear that Ruby's problems had little to do with school uniforms. 'Those schools are for the moneyed. You'll be out of your depth.'

The school was a homogenous community. It was a gift to all students and their privilege. Some parents were professionals, such as doctors, scientists and CEOs, but there were also bus drivers, bankers, fruiterers, salesmen. Our mothers were mostly homemakers. We'd visit each other and, regardless of income, our families lived similar lives, both in manners and conversation.

Cremorne Girls had a wonderful setting: rose gardens, tennis courts, bushes, shady trees for us to sit under and laugh and chatter and daydream. During French lessons, my mind's eye could see the branches at the top of a deciduous tree which stood next to the rose garden. In winter months, the branches could be seen more easily, divided, more delicate as they reached up, raising arms in praise of light.

From the science laboratory upstairs, there was Lloyd Rees's blue in the distance. Sydney Harbour. Sails hovered like moths. My spirit spent most of the time outside the laboratory.

When I first walked into the school library, it smelt and felt like a church. Instead of the minister sitting there on behalf of God, it was God Herself, Ms W. This was her church and it was as if she'd given virgin birth to each book. Borrowing a book was like asking for permission to take home one of her children.

One lesson, I accidentally dropped a book. Ms W's small stout body flew from her desk to the back of the room before there was even a chance to pick it up. She took the book, groaned and stroked it while examining it, checking for bruises. I returned it to the shelf, apologising all the while, but the apology was insufficient. She returned to her desk looking mortified at having to deal with such an ignoramus.

There was a whole shelf by, or about, William Shakespeare. My year six teacher, Mrs M, first introduced Shakespeare. Every Monday morning, she'd write in a column on the right-hand side of the blackboard, in the most beautiful script, a Shakespearean passage. She'd talk about it then dramatise it. We'd then recite it in one dramatic voice, in as sacred and as solemn a voice as we'd recite the Lord's Prayer or the Apostle's Creed. Our handwriting books were full of these passages. By the end of the week, we were expected to know the passage off by heart.

Mrs M used integration techniques long before they became fashionable. Also, at the end of every day, after we'd packed everything away, she'd prop herself on the corner of her desk and read to us for ten to fifteen minutes from *Wind in the Willows*, *The Cruel Sea*. It was a much loved and inspiring way to finish a day; a practice adopted in my own teaching years later.

In high school, we studied a Shakespearean play every term, alongside poetry and novels. We had large monthly English assignments in which Nanna always showed great interest. She liked to call in and have a cuppa on her way home from visiting friends before undertaking the final leg home. 'Show me what you've been up to.'

Cremorne Girls High School.

Always a bit overwhelmed by Shakespeare, I could rely on Nanna to make sense of the assignment. Her blue eyes would fire when she explained this and that, citing significant bits that would make good quotes.

My dear, vital grandmother, in her early eighties, shared with me, patiently, the beauty of Shakespeare's sonnets and she liked to reveal the irony and paradoxes hidden in witty dialogues and monologues in both the tragedies and comedies. She showed me how to read blank verse; how to hold the first thought line, suspensive-pause-like, and run with the intermediary, till the end of the piece, which, like the last line of a poem, would have closure.

My last year in high school we studied *Macbeth*. Nanna knew it well and liked to quote pithy pieces, revealing foibles and the common touch of kings and queens. Shakespeare was worth enduring at least for Nanna's sake if not for mine. In this very natural way, she taught me, at the knee so to speak, how to critically analyse, over a cup of tea and Jatz and cheese. I was unaware at the time that our literary feasts would soon cease.

Near the end of my last year at high school, just weeks before sitting for the Leaving Certificate, in 1961, Nanna was so weak she couldn't get out of bed. She could hardly talk. Her voice was threaded; guttural sounds intertwined. She coughed and coughed and had very bad breath.

Within weeks, Nanna was moved into a hospice in Wahroonga. When we visited her, she commented on the happy sounds of children she could hear playing at nearby Abbotsleigh Junior School. Little did we know then that, years later, I'd teach my heart out there. Whenever I visited Nanna, she'd struggle to ask, huskily, about my studies. We were kindred spirits.

Sadly, Nanna died from throat cancer on my last day of high school, the week before stu vac; her first grandchild to 'go on'. Nanna had been my greatest supporter, going against the consensus of opinion, which, in those days, was 'It's a waste of time letting her go on…she'll no sooner leave than she'll be getting married.'

The death of my dear paternal grandmother was my first intimate experience of loss and grief. At seventeen, I was still considered too young to go to funerals but I was there in my imaginings, which were probably more purple than what actually took place.

Not much happened during stu vac. Of a day, camped outside in the backyard with books, trying to escape the constant phone calls and visitors, I sat on a rug in the full sun and let the breeze blow study notes away. Didn't care. Made new notes. Didn't remember a word. It was simply something to do between long bouts of staring into the blue of the sky and wondering. Where was her person? They had Nanna's body but where was her person? I talked to her, cried; a novice in the world of grief.

*

'To weep is to make less the depth of grief.'
William Shakespeare
(Act II, Scene I, Line 85) *Henry VI,* Part III

Gran and Nanna.

14

Infinite Questions

My younger self was always confused when listening into women's conversations.

One day, a visiting aunt said to the women sitting around the table, 'Did you know B has fallen?'

'Fallen? Oh dear. Not again.'

'Won't she be happy.'

Everyone laughed.

How could they? Falling was no laughing matter. I hated falling. Fell all the time. Without irons on, skinning knees, elbows and burning palms on loose gravel and angry asphalt was the norm. It was said I not only tripped over my own shadow but everyone else's. It took Big Ears most of the conversation to realise 'falling' meant B was expecting a baby.

1958. Second year high school. Biology. Miss W, our adored teacher, explains a phenomenon whereby two eggs are fertilised in the womb but only one matures. On rare occasions, the other egg matures much later. Maybe it's a theory posed by someone in class or maybe a certain person isn't listening properly and only hears what she wants to hear.

This precious gem of information explains everything. Ruby often says she has no idea how this daughter of hers happened or who she's like. Now here's an answer: a proper answer, a scientific one. It's a delicate topic which requires much tact.

My weary mother often sighs at my after-school outpourings about some new discovery or newly acquired knowledge. So, advice to oneself – take it slowly. Definitely don't blurt anything out.

Around the back, Ruby stands at the clothesline. She struggles to fold a double-bed sheet. Kiss-kiss. 'Have a good day?'

'Yes, just wait till you hear.'

'Hold onto this, will you?'

I drop my ridiculously heavy port alongside the half-filled washing basket and grab one end of the sheet.

Ruby says, 'You arrived just in time.'

Is this the universe giving me a sign? I wave the sheet up and down.

'You're in a lively mood today.'

'You won't believe what I've –'

Ruby frowns and quickly pulls another sheet off the clothesline. We start folding in opposite directions.

'You're so left-handed,' she says.

'And you're so ambidextrous.'

We laugh until we're in synch. Laughter opens the door.

'Mum, I know why I came when I did.'

Her eyebrows arch. 'What are you –?'

'How I happened.'

'How what happened?'

'Me. You know how I was a mistake.'

'Don't say that.'

'You didn't plan for me, not really.'

'The timing could've been better, if that's what you mean.'

'Well, I think I know how it happened.'

Ruby's lips seal. She's patting the folded sheet into the basket more firmly than it deserves.

'Len and I might be twins. Not identical, obviously, but fraternal. I was probably a sleeping embryo.' These biological terms are designed to impress and represent authority.

'A what?'

'Incredible, isn't it?'

Ruby tugs at a startled white bed sheet. 'It never ceases to amaze me what nonsense they teach you at that school.'

'You were pregnant with me because –'

'Don't use that word.'

'What word?' I knew which word.

'You know very well. Here. Take this. Make yourself useful.'

I've annoyed my mother, again. She hands me the folded sheet. She's always about making yourself useful.

Ruby was only sixteen when she was sent to the city to work and she expects almost as much from us. I should've waited, but sleeping embryos and biology tipped the balance. It was never meant to spill over her. She nods towards the pile of sheets on the upturned wicket, the much dinted metal bucket.

'Pop those on the chair by the back door, will you.' She hurries inside carrying the professionally folded clothes in the large creaking cane basket.

Ruby's work as a laundress, during the parched Depression years, turned her laundering into an art. The clothes line was the place where, once, she shooshed me, told me to stand still and listen. We stood there listening. The washing whispered. It patted itself on the back and shadows danced. The wave of satisfaction on Ruby's face as we watched and listened suggested to me we were on hallowed ground. Was her serene expression because of some magical transformation taking place as we hung there on the clothesline? Was Ruby a gatekeeper, a guardian angel? Was the weekly washing a prayer of absolution for us?

Ruby's spiritual and professional attitude toward all things domestic meant she could've been, should've been, running the country.

Domesticity was universal, personal, especially noteworthy when it came to ironing shirts, sports shirts, billowing skirts, pin-tucked blouses.

Stan would boast, 'Nobody can light a candle to your mother when it comes to ironing.' Because of his dry-cleaning experience he had a unique insight into the quality of Ruby's work. It gave him a lifelong appreciation and admiration for his wife's fine finishes.

In contrast, I was an amateur with the iron. It was heavy work.

You had to press out creases in every corner of collars, cuffs, hankies, pillowcases and pillow shams. Fortunately, grace came one day in the form of an electric iron; a new wonder, time-saving, labour-saving wand. Compared to the old iron, this electric one only had to be waved over a garment. Soon I graduated. I had the grand privilege of ironing starched everything: tennis shorts, work shirts, school blouses, three-tiered petticoats. Many complaints were made about having to iron with such precision.

'If you're doing a job, it's worth doing well.'

The pathetic amount I ironed for my mother always seemed to please her. 'Thanks for that. Every little bit helps.'

I rest my chin on the freshly folded bed sheets on the top of the sun-kissed pile as we walk inside. We walk along the path, the broom-swept path, the ultra-smooth cricket pitch, my footsteps trying to follow in my mother's, all the while continuing to explain what might be meant by a sleeping embryo, with an urgent need to share this information. At fourteen, Ruby is everyone. She's my world, my centre, my sun. Stan is the funny man in the moon.

After a visit to the Australian Museum, when in primary school, we attended a lecture given by a lady who knew all about rocks and other things. From that lecture on, I developed an almost religious fascination for anything to do with the earth, rocks and fossils. It would be wonderful to be like that lady in the museum. Every day she shared wonders about rocks: actual history books, pasts immortalised, precious gems. My imaginary class sat obediently on the back toilet steps and listened to and observed all the pages of the *How and Why Book of Rocks and Minerals*. They were as fascinated as their teacher.

In high school, there was a discovery: I was science, biology. So was my family. We were water, cells, carbon, chromosomes. Biology was leading into a heady passionate world of infinite questions, questions about Family: blood types, bloodlines. Why blue eyes for the girls, brown for one brother and hazel for the other? Why was Gran so tall and my mother so small?

Both parents dismissed questions. 'Some people don't like talking about things like that. It's nobody's business.'

'But we're studying it at school.'

'Why? It's of no use.'

*

> Some family trees have beautiful leaves, and some have just a bunch of nuts. Remember, it is the nuts that make the tree worth shaking.
>
> Unknown

Ruby: my centre, my sun.

15

Turning Fourteen

Late one afternoon as Ruby stands by the stove and prepares dinner, she calls me over and indicates to stand close. 'I've got something to tell you.' She stirs the onion gravy. Her voice is breaking. She indicates closer, closer. 'I don't want your sister to hear. You're to promise not to tell.'

'I promise.'

The gravy is bubbling. It needs a stir but Ruby's stares past it. Shouldn't the spoon be stirring? Quickly the gas is turned down and the gravy is stirred.

My mother whispers, 'You're fourteen, old enough to know. I told your brothers when they turned fourteen.'

Fear rises. My arm reaches for hers but she stands still and stares into the gravy.

Ruby takes an immaculately ironed hanky out of her apron pocket. She presses it onto the tiny drops of perspiration on her top lip. 'You might not like what I've got to say.'

My mother appears to be shrinking. I've been taller than her for some time now. Nod-yes. Nod-no. Nothing will ever change my feelings.

'What I tell you might make you think differently about me. I want you to hear it from me and no one else. Gran is not my real mother.'

'Your real mother drowned, didn't she?'

'That's the thing. She didn't.'

'She didn't? Who is she?'

'She's one of your aunts.'

'Aunty who?'

'You won't like it when I tell you.'

It has to be Aunty Flora. They say she smokes like a chimney, something women in our family don't do. And they don't like her long red fingernails. She's tall and slim with flaming, wavy, red hair; the family film star.

Once I had a holiday with Aunty Flora and her parents, Uncle Will and Aunty Nell, in their large terrace in Moore Park. I didn't get homesick, not once, unheard of for me. When they asked if I'd like to stay a little longer, I said yes but Ruby felt it would be wearing out my welcome.

While there, Aunty Flora makes me a beautiful cowel-neck dress out of silky material. Its colours are sunshine and gold. When twirling around, its full skirt shimmers and shivers.

'Is it Aunty Flora?'

'Flora? Heavens, no. She's my cousin.'

'Sort of like Aunty Lil and Aunty Pat?'

'In a way.'

'Mum, just tell me, please.'

'You like working things out.'

It feels like the floor is slipping and I'm sliding into new territory. Need something to hold on to. Thinking. Thinking. An older aunt.

'Aunty Irie?' Auntie Irie always expects too much of Ruby. The way she sits by the kitchen table and criticises Ruby is hurtful and demeaning. Is this the reason why?

Every Sunday, Auntie Irie and Uncle Fred travelled from Quaker's Hill to see Mother. After Gran moved into the nursing home, they continued weekly visits to Mother, then they'd drive across to 68, have dinner then sleep soundly.

After their very late arrival, we'd sit down to a piping hot baked dinner, hot apple pie or lemon meringue. Once a month, after dinner, there was much for Stan to do. The dining table would be cleared. He'd have to work fast to get it all done because he had early morning starts. Bundles of unsold magazines from the newsagent section of

Fred and Irie's general store would be piled high on the table. Top strips, containing issue numbers, would be torn off and attached to forms which were sent back to the distributor.

The remains of the magazines were thrown away into our eager, outstretched arms. Every month, we feasted on delicious unsold magazines and comics like *Archie and Betty*, *Veronica and Reggie*, *Superman*, *Batman and Robin*, *Phantom*, tragic *True Romances*. We devoured them as did our neighbours.

Once all the magazines were sorted, Uncle Fred would collapse into Stan's comfy armchair, head back, mouth open wide and snore-roar.

Aunty Irie always sat in Gran's old chair, and, like her tired husband, she, too, would soon be head-drooped in a deep sleep. Meanwhile, Ruby worked her way through the deep cane basket and was always relieved when she glimpsed its bottom. It was usually piled high with mending, darning and ironing for Ruby, she being Irie's unofficial lady's maid and Irie being m'lady.

Sometimes on a cold blustery winter's night, Irie would say, 'Rube, aren't you cold? Go and put something warm on.' She never seemed to notice that her niece wore summer clothes in winter because her entire winter wardrobe was made up of one pleated woollen skirt, one winter coat and two knitted cardigans.

A neighbour gave Ruby the coat. It was beautiful, as if made for her. It was long, black, imitation fur. Its flared princess style floated around Ruby's trim figure and narrow ankles. Before she put it on, she'd rouge her cheeks then lightly powder-puff her face with Apple Blossom. She put on lipstick. Lastly, she'd tie a brightly coloured scarf around her neck. 'Just pray I don't have to take the coat off.' The coat gently swayed as Ruby walked down the hallway looking tall for such a small woman.

During winter visits, one of Irie's Cornelius furs would hang silently on our hallstand. The foxy one, with toffee eyes, permanently bared its teeth at anyone who dared walk past. The young fox should've been out in the backyard with Reynard stealing chooks. Had its long handsome brush ever wagged? Sometimes when daringly close, I could see clear, frozen tears along the rims of its glazed eyes.

'It's Auntie Irie, isn't it?'

'No.'

'No? Aunty Bessy?'

'No, not poor Bess, bless her.'

Bessie had several married children. She was widowed and had one daughter, Tuppy, living at home. Tuppy remained a child in her mind but had grown into a strong, moody woman.

'Does Tuppy have a missing chromosome?' I'd just learnt a little bit about what missing chromosomes could do and it sounded a lot like Tuppy. 'Is that why she –?'

'Ssssh. I don't want to hear you talking like that. It's none of our business.'

Which Aunt was left? Aunty Manie? It'd be lovely if it was Aunty Manie, although, if I wasn't supposed to like the person, then who could it be? It couldn't be Auntie Manie, who was sort of an unofficial grandmother anyway. I especially approved of the way she sometimes ate her dessert before the main meal. Whenever we had lunch or dinner there, she'd suggest we could do that, too, if allowed, but Ruby would give a look which meant we had to set our aunty a good example.

Eating dessert first was such a practical idea. There'd been a documentary at school about digestion, so there were a few technical terms that could help sway the argument. Ruby refused to accept any part of it. '

But Mum, having dessert first might make it easier to masticate. It might stimulate the digestive juices.' They were stimulated just thinking about it.

I also liked the idea that Aunty Manie and Uncle Tom had separate bedrooms, like royalty. Each room had its own personality. I dreamt of having my own room one day.

'Not something I'd like,' Stan said to Ruby one afternoon as we drove home from Drummoyne.

'I wouldn't either. But they seem none the worse for it.'

'I'll give you that. Not to my liking, though, so don't get any ideas.'

They laughed.

Auntie Manie made us all sorts of things. She made Wendy and me matching gingham dresses with white cross-stitch embroidered around the borders of the sleeves and around the hems of our very full skirts. I was *Anne of Green Gables* in that blue and white gingham dress but, unfortunately, grew out of it too soon.

The shorter women in the family often talked about my height.

'We'll soon have to put a brick on her head.'

'There's something unseemly about a woman being too tall.'

'She'll soon be as tall as Flora.'

'Or Nell.'

Gasps at that thought.

I said, 'I have no control over my height. It's in my genes.'

'Then don't wear jeans,' and we laughed.

But, at this stage, the wearing of jeans was no laughing matter. I grieved when I wasn't allowed to wear my beloved, faded green jeans any more. On becoming a fertile young lady at a modest twelve, I was not allowed to wear them. It was difficult to argue my case with someone who'd been brought up by her Victorian grandmother. The loss of jeans felt like I'd lost a layer of skin; a protective denim epidermis which had been peeled off for the sake of some female agenda.

'Is it Auntie Manie?'

'That'd be nice but I'm afraid not.'

'OK, Mum. I give up.

There's a pregnant pause. 'Rosie.'

'Rosie? You mean Aunt Gell? She's your mother?'

'Gran will always be my mother. She's the one who raised me.'

I dropped my jaw. 'Aunt Gell.' I swivelled my gaping mouth from side to side; Aunt Gell of the twinkling blue eyes, soft, beautifully, modulated voice; gentleness personified. 'Wow. I mean, what, why?'

Ruby hung her head.

'She's lovely, Mum.' I tried to put my arm around her but she shrugged me off.

'I'm all right.'

She didn't look it. 'That's so lovely, Mum.'

'You think so?'

I wanted to wrap my arms around my mother, assure her that I thought it was lovely but she moved away too quickly across to the kitchen table and into her old self.

'Here,' she said, 'you can finish laying the table and then tell the others it's time for tea.' She mashed the potatoes.

'I didn't think of Aunt Gell because –'

'Go on, you can say.'

'Say what?'

'Nothing. Now, just because I've told you, it doesn't change anything.' But it had, at least for me. Biologically speaking, I was now part of Aunt Gell and she a part of me and my mother and my brothers and sister. So why the intrigue? Why the secret? Why the shame?

'Why did you grow up with Gran and not Aunt Gell?'

'That's for another time, when you're older.'

We used to visit widowed Aunt Gell and Pop at Woy Woy. Their relationship was frowned upon by many family members because they were 'living in sin', not that we children knew. Pop used to keep us occupied with the gramophone. We'd queue up to wind it. In the meantime, we'd indulge in Aunt Gell's Devonshire tea and later eat one of her much-loved baked dinners.

When we were leaving, her eyes would fill. 'Don't leave it so long. You're always welcome.'

After Pop died, Gell moved back to Sydney. Whenever she stayed at our place, her goodnight hugs and kisses were always soft and warm. It was as if we fitted. When she listened to us, she'd lean slightly forward and nod, her blue-blue eyes swimming, smiling, connecting, as if to say, yes, yes, go on, I'm listening.

When Aunt Gell washed my hair, she'd rub it gently in direct contrast to Ruby, who scrubbed it so hard I used to warn her my head might fall off.

One afternoon as Aunt Gell dried my thick head of hair, she commented, 'Your mother used to have hair as thick as this, right down to her knees. She wore it in a long plait.'

'Don't tell her that,' Ruby said. 'She's always going on about wanting a plait.'

'It'd look nice.'

'All the goodness would go to her hair.'

'She's got the same hair as us.'

Ruby hurried back into the kitchen.

'Sorry,' Aunt Gell called out. 'I'm sorry.' Her eyes filled with tears.

I wondered why my thick hair would make my mother suddenly disappear and Aunt Gell cry.

Sometimes, Rosie shed a tear or two and Stan would say, 'Poor cow,' and he'd sidle up to her and joke and the next thing she'd be giggling and saying, 'Oh, Stan, there's no doubt about you.'

At fourteen, I'd learnt a little bit more about why Ruby often appeared lip-stitched, but remained unaware, for many more years, of how biology had slip-stitched her.

16
School by the Beach

Our annual holidays were always a month long. Stan and Ruby banked an amount every fortnight in the form of compulsory saving; an investment which yielded healthy dividends for family well-being.

It would be arranged that one of Gran's children would come and look after Mother while the family was away. Gran wanted to come too, and would sulk when Ruby started packing. Our family doctor assured the young mother that her grandmother would be fine.

Packing started weeks earlier. The large expandable tan leather port would be brought out into the living room and placed open across two spare dining chairs. As the weeks progressed, bundles of clean, well-ironed clothes would be professionally folded and added to the neat layers that were building up each day in the port. When it was full, someone sat on it while Stan latched and strapped the port full of hope. On the final day, it would be strapped to the roof of SB, our 1928 Dodge.

When it was time to leave, we'd kiss Gran and promise to send her funny postcards. We tried everything to take away her dejected look. Sometimes she came out and waved goodbye.

As we drove away, the first few minutes were always sad. Our parents would be blowing their noses and wiping eyes. Then they'd reassure the other.

'She'll be right.'

'I know. I think I got in everything she needs.'

'She'll be OK. Mum and Nell will pop in.'

'A month's a long time.'

Every year, Stan got five weeks' annual leave. The first four weeks we went on holidays. On the fifth week he did odd jobs: washing down the yellow, high-gloss kitchen walls, mending shoes, giving Gran's vegie patch a good going over, clearing his potato patch of last season's hidden treasures. He'd turn the soil over and over, banging out occasional lumps with his splendid flat spade. He'd rake the soil then sculpt small hills the length of the patch in readiness for the next sowing. He'd light a Ruby Red and stand in the shade of the back veranda. 'Not a bad job that, even if I say so myself.'

On holidays, our first stop was always at Mooney Mooney Creek. The picnic tablecloth would be spread out on one of the many picnic tables scattered throughout the park. Morning tea then cricket, chasing small crabs hiding in rocks beside the river while our parents walked and talked, shedding heavy layers of the past year. Packed up again we'd sing our way to The Entrance.

Guessing which of Mr Hungerford's cottages we'd be living in for the next month was exciting. He always gave us a cottage close to the beach. For the first few nights, it sounded as if waves were pounding against the house. There was the worry of a tidal wave coming while we were asleep. We'd learnt about them at school. Mummy said there was no such thing. Sleep came more easily after that.

There was a corner store which sold luscious lollies, ice blocks and ice creams. We were responsible for our own budgeting. Much of our pocket money was spent at the corner shop and at small gift shops in town. We also paid for our own small serving of hot salty chips of an afternoon when we walked into town.

The Butt children were always given a month's schoolwork to take away on holidays every late February/early March: *Betty and Jim Arithmetic* textbooks, English textbooks and books to read. After breakfast, on what would normally be a school morning, we'd sit around the holiday kitchen table and start the day with an hour's schoolwork. And there was no nonsense. We were expected to do our neatest and best work. If not, we had to do it again.

Ruby hovered nearby and Stan sat at the table supervising while doing the daily crossword. Anything we didn't understand was explained by either parent and if it was wrong we had to do it again. It was puzzling how just one hour a day's schoolwork always put us ahead of the rest of the class.

When the tide turned, we fished for flathead at the narrow entrance. At night we prawned when it was full moon at Long Jetty. We boated in a friend's rowboat that was kept nearby at their weekender. We played night tennis with visiting friends and relatives who came for short stays in Hungerford's cottages.

Back at school, it was great to see friends again. At first, I'd simply stare out the window, reliving the sound of waves breaking, the daring fun involved in bodysurfing with my father and the boys, learning to float on my back in the ocean pool, carving amazing castles in the sand. We were always happy to be home again but couldn't wait till next year's holiday.

Eventually, the cost of leasing a holiday cottage for a month every year, in an increasingly popular holiday spot, became prohibitive. By that time, most of us were independent and the boys were going on their own holidays. Our neighbours the Hugheses offered us a loan of their tent to see if we'd like camping. The camping ground Stan and Ruby first went to was directly opposite Hungerford's cottages.

The Entrance, 1950s.

17

Banyandah

Ruby was worried Stan would never want to camp again after they experienced all four seasons in four weeks: torrential rain, storms, wind, heat, humidity, along with the occasional sunny day.

It was such a successful baptism that they decided to buy themselves a twelve by twelve tent with kitchen annexe and accessories. We practised putting up the tent in our backyard. We polished our technique so well that we could set up everything in half to three-quarters of an hour. The first year, and every year after that, we'd leave home around 2 a.m. and, after many comfort stops, we'd arrive at Nambucca Heads on the north coast of New South Wales, twelve or so hours later.

Annual holidays meant it was time for me to apply for L plates, again. The routine was, every year, get Ls and brush up on driving skills before going away. At this stage, there was no urgent need for a licence because there was no need for me to own a car. By the time we got home after holidays, this learner driver would've driven hundreds of miles, in all conditions.

Driving north on our first year, we were unaware of the treacherous twists and turns on Bulahdelah Mountain. We stopped at the local park for a cuppa and sandwiches at its foothills. Stan was unaware we'd be driving more over the mountain than around it. He was tired from little sleep and suggested I take over for the next half hour or so or for however long.

As we crawled around sharp bends behind huge lumbering timber trucks, I said, 'Thanks very much, Dad.'

We giggled when we were confronted by huge timber trucks coming the other way where, on some corners, they had no alternative than to carve their way across the sharp curves as if they were heading straight for us.

'Pull over, Twerpo, as soon as you see a safe spot.'

But there was nowhere to stop and change drivers. I giggled nervously, or was it hysterically, once I realised we were on a mountain stuck with my learner driving skills, in a manual car whose handbrake needed remedial attention.

It was January 1962. We'd never been this far north before. We reached beautiful Nambucca Heads and turned into Banyandah State Forest; drove three miles on a well-graded dirt road until we reached the campsite where a private citizen had leased forty acres on the headland with access to the river/lagoon on one side and Pacific Ocean on the other. We were shown our site, which looked directly out to the Pacific Ocean. This was going to be a very different prospect to spending a month in one of Hungerford's cottages.

Lacking in sleep, we were keen to put up the tent, have a cuppa and kip. Our practice at putting up a tent proved to be invaluable and soon we were sitting at the camp table having afternoon tea. Our rest rolled into a solid sleep – that is, until early next morning when we were woken by a fellow camper.

'I popped over last night but you were all asleep. Rain'll be here sooner rather than later. Do you realise your tent's inside out?'

Erecting a twelve by twelve tent inside out is a quick and efficient way of meeting new neighbours. Soon, willing hands appeared. Action stations under a black sky. Everything out. Tent dismantled. Tent erected, this time right side out. With many a laugh at our novice ways, our new neighbours shared morning tea with us, sitting inside the tent on our small camp stools, watching the buckets outside fill with heaven-sent rain.

We interspersed lagoon or ocean days with substantial day trips. We'd all help make and pack a picnic basket full of sandwiches, fill a couple of Thermoses with hot water then leave with no idea where we were headed. We'd close the front gate of the State Forest. 'Left or right?'

One day, after a couple of hours driving north, we decided the Queensland border was reachable. No one in the car had been to another state before. Would it feel different after we crossed the border? Fact was, once the border was crossed, everything felt the same.

Rather than drive back to camp, we decided to stay in a bed and breakfast opposite the Tweed River, where the hosts emptied many a teapot with Stan and Ruby that night.

Another time, we headed for Dorrigo. One of the campers had told us about a beautiful rainforest walk.

Stan drove for a couple of hours then pulled over and said, 'You can take it from here, Twerpo.'

'Thanks very much, Dad,' I said when some time later we came to a sign announcing miles of winding road up ahead.

'Stop here,' Stan said. 'I'll take it.'

But being my father's daughter, driving was in my blood. Up and down and around Dorrigo Mountain was a narrow, twisting challenge.

The rainforest was so dense and steep that Stan got lost when he went to 'water the horse'. We cooeed till we finally found him, doubled over, hands resting on his knees, panicked, puffing, utterly out of breath. He couldn't walk the steep grade. This was the first time we witnessed the impact of emphysema.

In the tent at night, we were exposed to unfamiliar noises. We listened to the resident baritone frog serenade in the resonant water tank alongside the amenities block. We'd settle down, snug in our narrow stretchers and sleeping bags and listen to, and comment on, the sounds of the ocean, waves announcing, 'I've arrived.' We'd listen to owls hooting. Our ears became attuned to possible rustling sounds outside the tent. If it was due to rain, the snake trench around the tent needed to be freshly dug.

After lights out, and we'd be listening to the first drops of rain, Ruby would whisper, 'Stan, I hope that snake trench of yours is working.'

Stan'd whisper something and we'd hear giggling and Ruby would say, 'Behave yourself. You know what I mean.'

The first year was such fun we continued to return to Banyandah for years. Wet, windy or humid, we went out every day: swam in the lagoon, fished, collected shells, walked along different shorelines, bushwalked. Wendy and I used to take our air beds down to the lagoon and paddle up and down its small tributaries.

Necessity crept our annual holidays closer to Sydney. Our next camp was set up at the caravan park at Little Beach, Nelson Bay. Once again, we could fall asleep listening to the sound of breaking waves. The camp was nestled between the ocean and a protected bay. There were long wild flower bushwalks where soft, white, suede flannel flowers blanketed undeveloped land. There were protected places to swim, to meet friends for a day's picnic: Dutchies, Salamander Bay, Shoal Bay.

Stan and Ruby taught us how to grasp the lifetime found in every moment and to find joy, right there, in simple pleasures. Holidays by the sea and bushwalks were a tonic; filled us with gratitude and put hairs on our family's chest.

At times, the mystery and wonder of life overwhelmed. Lying in the tent in the cricket-filled night, we'd comment on the crescendo of cicadas and crickets and notice how the distant waves seemed to hold the melody. Did you hear that? They've all stopped at the same time. Who has the baton? Who can explain that great symphony that is life?

There were times when lying there, almost to the point of panic, as if outside myself, universal, I'd wonder how we became. It was difficult trying to reduce myself back into a tiny, tight-fitting, green sleeping bag. Was anyone else lying awake overawed by the vastness outside and the insignificance of our minuscule selves inside a canvas twelve by twelve?

18

Spring

I'm the girl in blue swimmers on Manly Beach
I'm hugs
I'm kisses
I'm blossom
I'm spring

1962. Hot summer's night. Saturday night. Dancing. North Sydney Police Boys' Club, Falcon Street, North Sydney. The queue turned its collective head when Stan parked the car outside the main entrance. It watched my friend and me struggle to control our effervescent skirts and petticoats as we climbed out the back of the FE Holden sedan.

'We'll pick you up at twelve,' Stan said.

Ruby spoke in capital letters. 'SHARP.'

'Thanks for driving us,' Susie tinkled.

Susie was the one Ruby feared would lead her daughter astray any day now. She had two older sisters who were nurses and they taught me things like how to shave one's legs and under one's armpits. Ruby said she'd never heard of anything so ridiculous. There were lessons on how to fold hankies into triangles and use them to plump up limp bra cups, creating necessary curves, in our minds, at least.

They also taught me there was another reason for going to the beach and it had nothing to do with swimming. It was all about the Tan. Method:

• salt skin regularly by dipping oneself into surf, remembering that salt is an essential ingredient for crackling

- rub in generous quantities of oil
- put hat on head and lie on towel
- rotate frequently
- repeat this process every twenty minutes.

When tanning with friends, we'd lie on the silken sands of Manly, Fairy Bower, Queenscliff, Harbord or Balmoral beaches. Regardless of my basting and conscientious roasting, I never attained the crackling tan of Susie and her sisters. On tanning days, it was best to swim discreetly, whereas when swimming with family, we'd stay in the water so long our fingers and toes would wrinkle. But tanning days were for roasting.

Back home, at the cool end of day, Ruby would insist on a hot shower to treat sunburn. 'The hotter the better. It'll take out the heat.' It seemed to create more, but she insisted.

As soon as she left the bathroom, the water would be turned down to lukewarm but still the skin sizzled. Patting steam dry was an impossibility. Layers and layers of Nivea cream were applied to face, bright red legs, arms and feet.

'More fool you,' Ruby would say as she rubbed in dollops of chilled Nivea over my tender back and shoulders. There'd be loud complaints and much squirming. 'Stand still,' she'd say. 'I'm hardly touching you. You've brought this on yourself, you know.'

This particular February night was a debut of sorts. It was my first night-time social outing outside of church fellowship activities. Stan and Ruby were attending the monthly 2CH dance just around the corner on the first floor of North Sydney Council Chambers. Finally, I'd been allowed to go to the Police Boys' Club dance with Susie because my parents found out it was well supervised and an alcohol-free zone.

Light-coloured clothes worn that night were meant to accentuate the tan but compared to Susie's mine looked decidedly anaemic.

Ruby said, 'We'll wait until you're inside.'

'No, don't worry. Look at the line.' And, besides, there were no other parents hovering.

Ruby glanced at the long line and turned her head towards Stan and mumbled something.

He leant across and said, 'Make sure you don't leave the building.'

'Why would I?' A perfectly innocent question. That's what worried them.

Only months earlier, my brother Len had ribbed me at the dinner table. 'Sis, what's a virgin have for breakfast?'

'How would I know. Why, what's a virgin?'

'Mum, Dad. Did you hear that?'

It was obviously a trick question. I wondered aloud. 'There's the Virgin Mary.' I knew that meant Jesus had a heavenly father but as for the mechanics –

'Do something, quick. Mum, Dad. Tell her what a virgin is.'

'That's enough,' said Ruby.

Eighteen-and-a-half-year-old Len stared at me. 'At seventeen, you should know.'

'Why? What's a virgin got to do with anything?' How could a seventeen-year-old young woman, who'd almost finished high school, be expected to know everything? How could someone who ate Vita Brits for breakfast be expected to know that her petticoat of innocence was hanging well below the rising hemline of the progressive sixties? And how was she to know she was blossom; she was spring?

We waved goodbye to my parents, joined the queue, bought tickets and walked upstairs and stood on the outer edge of the dance floor amongst others. We looked at each other. What happened now? How did we become part of this rhythm and dance? We stood and watched. There were mating sounds between saxophone and drum. It was toe-tapping time.

'Would you like to dance?' he said, so tall I could hardly see his eyes.

He was open country in manners, his voice double malted caramel. The band was sassy, the heartbeat strong. Our feet soon found the earthy beat: quickstep, Canadian three step, Pride of Erin, jazz waltz. He was easy to follow.

Eddie had graduated from Armidale Teachers' College and had recently arrived in Sydney. This was his first teaching appointment at a local high school. He'd come to the dance with a college friend.

How could I tell this absolute doll of a freshly sown teacher that, only recently, I'd missed out on getting a teachers' college scholarship? I couldn't. Hadn't come to terms with it myself. My spirit was still spinning because, months earlier, I'd moved myself into a fictional teachers' college. Although I'd passed all subjects in the Leaving Certificate, my ignorance in choice of subjects made all the difference.

I was sure this confident, young graduate, who'd made it to centre-stage, wouldn't be so ignorant. This articulate breath of fresh air made me feel a little tongue-tied. Here he was, and here I was, a good church girl, quickstepping with high-heeled missionary zeal. As we danced, 'Moon River' pulled a very strong tide. It swelled and flooded its banks. I'd never danced with Zeus before.

The night spun too soon. We arranged to meet the next day. I'd catch the 144 Manly bus at Crows Nest and he'd pick it up at Balgowlah.

Susie and I hurried out to meet my parents, who were waiting in the car outside.

'So, how was it?'

'Great.'

'Did you meet anyone you know?'

'No. But I've been asked to go to the beach tomorrow. I'll still take my Sunday school class but I won't go to church.'

'We'll see what your father says about this.'

'I agree with whatever your mother says.'

'Thanks very much. You're no help. I'm not happy about this, you know.'

I, too, was a little worried now that I was sitting in the back seat of reality. My friend had encouraged me to go but she'd left school a couple of years earlier and, although she was younger, she always seemed more mature and sophisticated and wore her hair in a French bun. But I really wanted to go to the beach. It was my home away from home. Besides, I liked this country boy. I liked the way we spun out as we danced, all the time talking. He was lighting up a whole new corner of my brain.

'But, Mum, remember you said I could go out with boys once I left school? That was three months ago. I'm seventeen. I've got a job. For heaven's sake, when can I go?'

'No need to speak to your mother like that.'

'What I meant was for you to go out with someone you know.'

It was true. I hardly knew him but, in a way, I felt I did. He was quick-witted and we shared the same sense of the ridiculous.

'He's from the country like you.' I hoped this might influence the unhappy, highly influential front passenger.

'You can see him at the dance next week. Get to know him first. Just because you meet someone doesn't mean you have to go out with them.'

'We're only going to the beach.'

Ruby turned to Stan. 'Are you going to let your daughter go out with a complete stranger?'

'I suppose it's got to happen sometime.'

'And what if you catch the wrong bus? What if he doesn't turn up? What will you do then?'

'I'll catch another bus home.'

Friday nights were fellowship nights. Saturday night was prayer meeting. The occasional meeting was attended but we much preferred to go to the local Methodist youth club. It had a four-square programme: activities, dancing, singing and a devotional.

Once a month, on Saturday nights, my friends and I went with my parents to the 2CH dance. Long trestle tables lined the perimeter of the hall. Families and friends brought supper and drinks with them and soon transformed the room into a colourful series of mini-feasts.

Sometimes, one of my parents would take us onto the highly polished, well-sprung dance floor and would teach us some old-time dancing, the swing waltz or similar. They were good teachers too, and light on their feet and graceful.

During the Depression, Stan and Ruby won occasional prizes for ballroom dancing. Ruby loved the competitions but Stan didn't.

Ballroom dancing was seen to be a necessary accomplishment for young ladies and gentlemen. Attendance at dancing classes in sixth class, on the first floor of Chatswood Town Hall, were necessary. As soon as I passed first grade, I left because my hands were too sweaty and so were the equally nervous boys. Ruby was disappointed.

In my final year of high school, a partner was needed to accompany me to the school formal.

Both brothers organised different partners. 'All you have to do is choose.'

This pressure made it worse. Not even the beautiful dress we'd put on lay-by could tempt me to change my mind.

'If you're quite sure,' Ruby said as we climbed off the bus at Crows Nest and walked back down Willoughby Road. As we were about to enter the dress shop, Ruby stopped. 'It's not too late. You can change your mind.'

'It's really not important…some others aren't going.' At least, I hoped that was so.

The shop assistant recognised us and refunded the deposit. She and my mother exchanged unreadable looks. She unpacked the lay-by out of its box and placed the slender black velvet shoulder straps onto a hanger as we walked out the door. She teased out the full underskirt of taffeta and billowed the outer skirt of soft white chiffon. Its tiny black velvet polka dots looked like they were dancing in the late afternoon sun.

The shop assistant hung it in a prominent position, as you first walked in the door. 'If you change your mind, darling, you'll have to be quick because it's a real sweetheart.'

Part of me was left behind as we walked out the door. To think it'd almost been mine. We crossed the road into the glaring sun.

Ruby looked glum. It seemed there was some preordained script I was meant to follow. Who wrote this script? Added to this puzzlement was my embarrassment with boys. It would've been so much easier to be carefree and comfortable with them as some of my friends were.

Even my younger sister knew things about them I didn't.

'How do you know these things?'

She'd laugh. 'You just do.'

But I didn't.

The dress needed to be cancelled for another reason. The formal was going to cost more than the dress. There was talk of evening accessories. Some friends were concerned about length of evening glove, type of stole, size of evening bag, matching shoes. Added to this was the cost of two tickets. It was my belief that these expenses would be well outside the family budget.

Ruby kept a strict budget book and it rarely showed a deficit. She should've been running the country. We lived within our elasticised means. One of her favourite sayings was 'You can be as rich as a king if you live within your means. The best things in life are free, you know.'

As soon as we started earning money we, too, had to keep a budget book, which was occasionally scrutinised. Allowances had to be made for unexpected expenses, not just the known ones.

My long-suffering mother and I stood under the shaded awning waiting for the bus to arrive. We stood together in a vibe of disappointment. From where we were standing, I could see my hope hanging inside the doorway of the shop. Someone would soon come and claim its shining delight.

I turned to my mother, who stood too quietly. I needed to close the distance between us. I wanted to relieve her disappointment. 'Anyway,' I said, 'we couldn't really afford it, could we?'

Ruby clutched her handbag. 'It was a lay-by. We'd have managed.'

My decision not to attend the school formal took me another step closer to becoming the already suspected family eccentric, as I was referred to by some, supposedly out of earshot. Not the black sheep. There were no black sheep to speak of but falling short of family social expectations did challenge the norm.

'You're different to others. I think it's because everything comes so easy to you. You don't appreciate –'

'Mum. Easy? It might look easy but –'

'You know what I mean.'

'No, I don't but I do know the boys can say or do whatever they like. How come I'm not even allowed to say what I mean? What's so easy about that?'

'Enough's enough. Right?'

No, it wasn't right but Ruby had had enough. I didn't want to annoy her. She might withdraw her affection and no cause was worth that.

Anne, Manly beach girl, 1962.

19
First Date

Sunday morning. Sunday school. St Stephens, Willoughby. Small chairs belonging to my five-year-old students are packed away. We make a big circle and join hands in the Sunday school hall and sing in our heartiest of voices.

> 'Sunday School is over
> and we are going home.
> Goodbye, goodbye,
> we will be kind and true…'

As I hurry along the shaded southern path behind the church, Miss D is standing at the other end. She doesn't know that at this stage my spirit has already flown ahead and is sitting on a bus. It'd be difficult to explain the need to catch up with myself.

'Good morning, Anne.'

'Morning, Miss D.'

'Would you mind handing out attendance stickers after church today?'

'Sorry, Miss D. I can't today.'

She coughs. 'Someone said you went to a dance last night.'

'Yes.'

'What do your parents think about that?'

'They took me. Sometimes they go to the 2CH dance around the corner so they took me and picked me up.'

How would she feel if she knew my parents taught us the reverse waltz around the dining room table? What would she think of Wendy and me pushing back that same table to make room for our wild gyrations to Crash Craddock's 'Boom Boom Baby'?

Would she ever be able to understand that, in our family, dance was a form of celebration, fun, fellowship? It wasn't a sin. It was rhythm, expression, communication. At family parties, we'd sing and dance, performers all. Of course, we had favourite requests: Stan reciting 'The Little Toy Soldier' covered in dust, sturdy and staunch he stands...'; Aunty Nell singing, 'I'm a Little Fireman, short and stout...' We'd laugh so much as she desperately tried to assist the fireman ring the bell and put out the fire; Oscar material.

Ruby was a favourite, too. She'd stand, look at everyone very seriously, hands clasped in front of her as if she was about to recite; feet together. In a high-pitched, quavering baby's voice she'd sing, 'I'm forever blowing bubbles.' Encore. Encore. The pianola played and we were the chorus. We'd sing harmonies: 'Daisy, Daisy...', 'You are my sunshine, my only sunshine...', 'Show me the way to go home, I'm tired and I want to go to bed...' The evenings always ended too quickly. We'd collapse into comfy armchairs or lie on the floor out of sheer exhaustion from laughing so much and from having outperformed ourselves, once again.

I indicate to Miss D the need to pass. Our cheeks are red.

She looks down at the stickers. 'I won't keep you but I do hope to see you at prayer meeting next Saturday.'

Worried about missing the bus, I race home and change. Part of me stays with Miss D. It was uncomfortable feeling her disappointment. She's a loving soul; well-intentioned, devoted to her Lord. As I look out the bus window, there are questions: is this running away from the likes of Miss D running away from God? I hope not.

When the bus arrives at Balgowlah, my new friend stands at the bus stop and fear of Ruby's words – 'He's just as likely not to turn up, you know' – subside. He's here and he walks along the aisle of the bus with his head bowed in the manner of the very tall.

As the bus gathers speed, he leans forward and points to the left, to a dark brick house. 'That's where I live, in the garage out the back. 'The Balgowlah Hilton,' Hylton being the name of his landlord. We laugh and his blue eyes fire.

We spread our towels on the welcoming sands of Manly Beach near the shade of Norfolk pines. There's no script for this. It's my first outing without family or friends. Ruby's right. This young man's a stranger.

Even so, I feel at home with this lean, lithe, healthy nineteen. He's a buzzing bundle of energy that sends out sparks whenever he sits, stands, rolls this way and that. He's so much like the waves in the background: perpetual motion.

We don't stay in the water too long. The surf is strong. Instead we bake and walk and talk. Until now I've heard much about the lush beauty of his northern paradise. At times, it seems to overwhelm the beauty of where we are, these inviting sands, these welcoming fun-loving waves of azure. I offer to show him Fairy Bower. As we walk, he says he plans to go back north to live one day. I hope not. I'm warming to his breaking waves of laughter, his witty repartee and sensuous line of limb.

At the powder-blue end of day, we walk back to his place via a small bay where sea creatures shelter in rocks. My companion overflows with scientific information. How can he remember such detail? I studied these creatures in biology in recent years and had already forgotten most of their names.

It's fun kneeling down, peering at these wondrous creatures, observing the instinctual everyday tidal movements, mostly unseen; God in the rhythm, in the tide, in the limpet, in the exuberance of long warm arms and legs so close to me.

We clamber over rocks and stroll past Forty Baskets Beach. We walk along paths until we finally reach his place. He takes me to the Balgowlah Hilton and all the while Ruby sits on my shoulder. 'Young lady, get yourself home right now.'

Of course, E is a gentleman. We have a cool drink in the main house and he walks me to the bus stop and before the bus comes we speak about meeting at the dance the following Saturday.

It was a long week. I decided to sew a new outfit. I bought material during the lunch hour and, at night, drafted patterns; a violet of iron-boat-neck, three-quarter-sleeved top in small print. The skirt was box pleated in a mid tone of salmon with a wide buckle on a matching belt.

Over the next few weeks, Eddie and I shared new experiences. For me, new ways of thinking, challenges to past beliefs and practices. For him, there were new places. We went to the Domain on Sunday afternoons and, in amongst the jostling crowds, we listened to speakers. It was rollicking. Bluey, aka Big Red, screamed hellfire and damnation. Then we'd amble along to the gentle Ada and her tambourine.

> 'Jesus loves the little children,
> All the children of the world…'

We lingered in the art gallery and sat close on Mrs Macquarie's Chair. From there we could soak up Lloyd Rees's celebration of salt and sail. We'd stroll through the botanic gardens; the city's sensitive soul. We'd lie on its lush velvet heart and listen to its pulse.

I was in love with the city and with this young man's blue-eyed-blue-fired universe, lost in gentle hugs. When we kissed, it was sheer phosphorescence.

May school holidays meant my friend would head home to his beloved Tweed Heads. I was going to miss his turbo-charged laughter, his detailed chatter, his warm, telling lips.

20

The Change

Holidays passed. Not a word. No phone calls. It could mean only one thing. Saturday-night activities were rearranged so as not to face the embarrassment of rejection. I went to the pictures with friends. After some weeks, we headed back to the dance.

I danced with a mutual friend who said, 'How's Ed?'

'I don't know.'

'Must've been a bad accident.'

'Accident?' I sought out his college friend.

'I thought you knew. He's pretty down. Give him a ring.'

Ring? Our phone was in the living room. It was impossible to hold a private conversation. Whenever our phone rang, conversations in the living room stalled and you could hear ears flap.

And another problem. Nice girls didn't ring boys. Walking down to the corner post office, I could hear my mother, on my shoulder, once again, scolding me. 'He should be ringing you.' At arm's length, I put in pennies and dialled. When he answered, I blushed. He said he didn't feel like going out but, yes, he'd like to see me. We arranged a visit the following Sunday.

He opened the front door. There before me were drooped shoulders, pained, faded eyes. He looked at me sideways, showed terrible scars. Skin burnt at the sight. These scars were a survivor's badge of attitude and courage. They deserved to be kissed.

As a front-seat passenger, he didn't remember much about the car running off the road. He'd been thrown out of the car and it rolled over him; energy crushed, comatised. This was definitely not the same vibrant, young man who'd so tenderly kissed me goodbye a few months earlier.

The sun shone on us for a while but this time there were long shadows. The scars served a change. There was a cool resolve in his weathered, leathered recovery. Elvis sang, 'You acted strange and used the change…'

The longest shadow of my friend's cool resolve had nothing to do with the accident. Initially, he'd come to Sydney to study for a science degree.

I puzzled. 'If you're already a qualified teacher, why do you need a degree?' I knew nothing about the difference between a diploma and a degree.

Missing out on a teachers' college scholarship, because of a misunderstanding about subject choice, was hard for me to accept, because I knew its history.

The maths mistress, also our careers adviser, had appeared at the door of our English class one day. She was looking for me. 'Anne, do you realise you haven't chosen maths for fourth year?'

'Yes, Mrs H.'

'Drop anything but maths.'

At that time it would've been too embarrassing to explain that to go on at school, for the final two years, only useful subjects were allowed. There'd been pressure from some older extended family members, telling me how selfish it was wanting to stay on at school. 'Should be out earning money, helping your mother, not worrying about books.' They could be heard pressuring Ruby, too. Pragmatism was going to be inevitable when choosing subjects.

We went through the columns of subject choices together.

'Needlework. You'll always need to know how to sew.'

Tick.

'But, Mum, we already know how to sew.'

'We have some fine needlewomen in our family. Aunt Gell, as you know. Now, home economics.'

'Did that in first year and hated it.'

Tick. (Mind you, the practical knowledge gleaned in home economics has been invaluable. The skill of knowing how to prepare a three-course dinner within the confines of a tea towel should never be under-rated.)

'Art?'

'I love art. Mrs S says –'

'It won't put food on the table.'

'Mrs H says I have to take maths.'

'You're already good at that.'

French went, too.

So maths, French and art were dropped.

Economics was allowed because it sounded practical, probably a bit like home economics. Maybe it'd teach me something about budgets. We both knew how important budgets were. And, in a way, it did. It turned out to be domestic, universal, political, a bird's eye view of all things economic.

When choosing subjects, I assumed every subject had equal value. I knew nothing about subject scaling or about getting into the right scholarship queue which would admit you into teachers' college or university. I didn't know that subjects which could be studied at university ranked higher than subjects studied at TAFE. This misunderstanding still exists amongst parents and students today. It's why many independent schools offer very few low-ranking subjects. It ensures that their students find themselves standing in the right tertiary queue.

My parents weren't professionals. They didn't know about queues. Neither did I. All I knew was universities were for doctors, scientists and engineers. Colleges were for teachers and TAFE for apprentices. Nurses lived in and trained on the job while others went to secretarial college.

21
Punch-drunk

In the early sixties, not long out of school, I came perilously close to getting drunk. It was a Cremorne Old Girls' reunion. My friends and I were very new old girls.

We especially enjoyed the delicious punch which we drank from tall, very thirsty glasses. The speeches were the most entertaining I'd ever heard and, although we were hushed on a couple of occasions, it didn't stifle our enthusiasm. Our cheers encouraged anyone who looked remotely like a potential speaker. Yes, the speeches were great. I remember that.

As we left the restaurant at the close of ceremonies and stepped out into George Street, we were accosted by a fierce gust of fresh air. Usually I welcome fresh air but not on this occasion. It hit me and some of my friends so hard that we almost fell over. But we reminded ourselves we were Cremorne Old Girls. We could do anything we set our minds to, so we formed a formidable crocodile line which, by the way, I recommend as an effective combatant against unsuspecting late night winds. We struggled valiantly forward until a coffee lounge appeared out of nowhere.

We were settling down for a decent chat, shoes kicked off, chairs well back, because the coffee kept spilling, when the proprietor asked us to leave. He tried to tell us it was closing time. Come in Spinner. Arms linked, we headed for Wynyard. I hope I drank my coffee.

I know we successfully arrived at the bus terminal because I caught the right bus home. I remember crossing the Harbour Bridge and all the fond farewells at various bus stops. I have a vague memory of an elderly gentleman sitting nearby and he scolded me while I giggled like a schoolgirl.

After getting off the bus at my usual stop, I vividly recall the rush of exhilaration at the late-night freedom. Not a car in sight. For the first time ever, I walked up the middle of the usually busy main road. It looked like a dark velvet ribbon and it led me home.

I was surprised to meet my mother at the front gate, but, as she said, she knew I was on the last bus because she heard me coming. She recognised my laugh as I made my way up the road. I can hear her now asking me if I had a good time as we walked arm in arm up the front steps. She suggested it was best not to disturb my father, so I headed off down the hallway using the hallstand as my guide.

Eighteen. Ground-breaking documentary film, in full technicolor, showing the real life birth of a baby. I expected my mother to be impressed that I was going to be brave enough to see it because in her day there were no such opportunities.

'You're far too young. Your time will come soon enough. Fools rush in, that's all I've got to say.'

Her first birth story was 'I was seven months pregnant and your father was rubbing warm olive oil over my swollen tummy because the skin was itching. It helped and was said to prevent stretch marks. The bigger I got, the more worried I was about my navel. I asked your father why it wasn't getting any bigger. I thought the naval opened up and that's where the baby came out. Your father put me right, of course.'

S and I saw the film after work. The big screen magnified, zoomed, loomed, and some parts were only caught with half an eye. The lower half of a woman's body was unknown territory. Childbirth exploded on screen. Mother Nature was an orchestration. Symbols crashed. Violins screamed. Bloodied raw emotion, rhythm, pain, maths, music, colour crescendoed. We were watching the birth of a new universe.

Did this happen every time? Always? Happening right now? Youch.

Unfortunately, the film didn't explain the metaphorical arrows, but, then again, they might've been shown during times when my eyes were closed.

As soon as the lights came on, S and I looked at each other and giggled, nervous hysteria, at what lay ahead. We avoided looking at any patrons as we silently filed out of the theatre and headed home filled with wonder and fear.

'Mum, you didn't tell me. It's unbelievable.'

'Shouldn't be showing things like that.'

'I don't think I'll ever have a baby if that's what happens.'

'See, that's what I mean. You're not ready. When it happens, it'll be natural and you'll soon forget all about the pain.'

The only pain related to childbirth that Ruby ever mentioned was the time, after the birth of her fourth child, the nurse accidentally cleaned her recently stitched vaginal tear with methylated spirits.

It was said that universities weren't safe places for young women. They were hotbeds; full of undesirables. Headlines said so. They were seen by many parents, such as mine, as having a bad influence on young women. There was Sydney University: the Push, promiscuity, drugs, anarchy.

Stan was firm. 'No daughter of mine is going to any university to learn how to become a communist or a nincompoop.'

Mrs H, the career counsellor, had been annoyed when I handed back some unsigned forms. 'Why did they send you here if it wasn't for you to go on to tertiary education?'

I couldn't tell her that they hadn't wanted me to come in the first place.

'You're well suited to further education, particularly communications.'

Ruby's response was 'Communications? What sort of job is that? Who's ever heard of –'

I was hoping she might tell me because I was too shy to ask in the interview.

E's steely resolve to study part-time at University of NSW made him even more of a threat to Stan and Ruby's daughter. And his decision required a declaration. Things had to change. And there was more. This boy was not for marriage. I should go out with others.

Who'd said anything about marriage? I was hardly out of school. And, surely, the whole dynamic of society was changing. My friend's proclamation was unnecessary, irritated me, but I didn't have the agency to debate the issue and if I tried, it was as if I wasn't believed, which annoyed me even more.

Marriage involved overwhelming matters of wifely and housekeeping duties. I'd learnt that in home economics. I wasn't ready for that. Besides, I'd only just started making my own bed.

22

Twenty Per Cent Discount

Now that my teaching dream was over it was difficult to find direction. Also, on the social scale, if you weren't engaged or about to be engaged at my tender age, you were considered too fussy.

But the role of women in history was changing. Why the uproar? Why the need for a women's movement? What was meant by suffragettes? Equal rights, even in marriage, seemed to be the crucial issue. So where did all this come from? Where was it going? The history of women didn't look good. I certainly didn't want to be somebody's property: a possession like a handbag, a hostess, an asset-wife listed alongside assets of old, like the house cow, or be a necessary rung in the ladder of a husband's career trajectory, the one who had to be seen to be the head of the house, the provider.

'I would love to have kept working,' Ruby said in hushed tones, one day. 'But I couldn't do it to your father. He said he wouldn't have his wife going out to work. He'd have been very unhappy if I –'

Marriage was a pragmatic institution; good for the economy. Economics taught me that. Yes, but was it good for those within the institution? Was it good for those who had to stay, until death did them part, regardless? Wasn't that an irresponsible thing to ask of imperfect beings? At this point in my life, I'd have much preferred to stand in bare feet on ice.

I missed my sometimes-friend. At times he'd ring or arrive unexpectedly. On one occasion, I had the temerity to ask if he'd mind ringing earlier in the week to organise these outings. My request to ring earlier was monumental. It was equal to tying a hawser to his hawse-hole. Other dates did ring earlier to ask if I'd like to go to a ball or to the pictures, on a picnic with friends, a car rally, harbour cruise, dinner, theatre, dancing.

Although E was my photosynthesis, and a subliminal influence, I was realistic enough to know the direction in which we were headed.

'I had this dream,' he said. 'You were lying high up in a glass coffin. I put orchids all around you…woke up bawling. Couldn't stop.'

It explained his conflict regarding our close bond and his fear of it thwarting his ambition. I was touched he'd cried. I understood, but it made no difference. The dream orchids were a loving gesture. I cried too.

'I can't help it if you had a bad dream that I died. Is it any reason –?'

'Forget about me.'

'I will. I'm sick of the way you carry on.' And I went out with others.

While our break-ups were hard, they were an additional weight to the already heavy losses around that time: missing out on a teachers' college scholarship, fretting over the losses of both my beloved grandmothers, Nanna and Gran, who died within six months of each other.

Panic attacks peaked in the bus when I was travelling to work.

Ruby said, 'It's your nerves playing up,' so she made an appointment with our local GP.

He warned me that if I didn't make a plan in the next week or so, he'd put me into hospital.

I enrolled in a course with International Correspondence Schools (ICS): 'Psychology, the study of Mental Life.' It ensured I was over-occupied: assignments, work, netball, friends, family, fellowship. No more panic attacks.

As more friends announced engagements, it was polite to be happy for them, but they were so young, so young. One couple decided to open a joint bank account after their first date. This was terrifying news. How to congratulate the couple's affirmative action? Why the rush? Why set relationships in concrete so early? Didn't they want to leave first footprints on fresh dew of a new dawning? But then again, it seemed that, in my crowd, I was the one out of step.

Insight was surfacing, stepping into unpopular territory, questioning inequality and questionable rights in the dominant patriarchal institutions. Fear flooded as each question shifted the very foundation on which I stood, causing a seismic, psychological shift.

I'd been working as a share clerk for two years. The job was meant to be temporary. My friend had rung during the last week of the Leaving Certificate exams. She worked at PT in the city, and said the company was looking for recent school leavers who'd studied economics. 'They're holding interviews on Monday. Would you like me to arrange one?'

It sounded more interesting than my current part-time job at Grace Bros, where I worked for two years of a Saturday morning in the Chatswood store, and I fully expected to be working there during school holidays and while at teachers' college. I'd recently been promoted from Ladies' Underwear to Ladies' Shoes. It added an extra shilling to Saturday morning's pay. Fitting shoes was preferable to fitting brassieres, which was an intimate, inappropriate job for a schoolgirl. Pleasing large-breasted customers as we sought to find the most comfortable, most suitable cups was a skill honed by the more buxom, mature members of staff. This new job opportunity would, hopefully, be less confronting than being in close quarters to hot crotches and sticky stockinged feet.

Two young men and myself were interviewed. We started work the following Monday. I'd sat for my economics exam the week before the interviews. I vividly remember walking out of the exam empty of anything economic. Couldn't have done the paper again. Left everything behind. What if I failed? Would they sack me? Should I tell my friendly workmates about future plans or keep quiet and start training?

Two years later, there was a promotion: a fully fledged share clerk, no longer in training. My immediate boss had left for overseas. Now there was my own desk and a typist. First job was to format a set of pro-formas to save time. Except for business names and amounts, almost every handwritten letter sent to a stockbroker or company share clerk was almost the same. They weren't going to be broken-hearted if they didn't receive a beautifully handwritten letter like the ones my boss used to send.

Even though it was a privilege to be there, I didn't want to be there, but was. I often viewed myself as if from eagle height, sitting in the middle of the city, in a big brick building, on the third floor, at a desk, signing transfers of shares from deceased estates.

I stayed on because of my workmates. I admired their grit. If I'd gone straight to college, I would never have appreciated the importance of humour and cooperation, essential currencies in any office, no matter how frantic or humdrum. I'd never have appreciated the lyricism of typists at work. Boredom provided me the opportunity to observe different types of beauty in my co-workers' faces, sense their God, get to know their inner child, discover that everyone was someone's son or daughter, no matter how old.

I joined the works netball team and played every year, meeting with other netballers from insurance companies and banks. One season, feeling desperate to distract myself from myself, I joined three netball teams, playing defence or assistant defence: C grade at work, B grade for a Paddington Twilight team and reserve for A reserve at Moore Park. At least, chasing a ball gave me a goal.

Most co-workers in the office were getting engaged, were already engaged or were in recovery from a broken engagement.

It's lunchtime. My friend and I race along Pitt Street. We're trying to beat the clock. We travel at group speed. We're carrying towels from DJs. Specials. Twenty per cent discount. In the locker room it's show and tell. I can't mirror the exuberant oohs and aaahs when the towels are held up high. Eyes sparkle as bright as any diamond. The camaraderie about the towels smothers me. Pack the towels into the locker and hide head in its cool darkness for a few seconds. Mouth a silent, private scream. Air is fresher in here, not as dense as the passionate, delusional hope being invested in discounted towels.

Ruby admires the towels. We both love beautiful linen. Then it's time to wonder aloud about delusions, illusions and unrealistic dreams vested in discounted towels.

'I don't understand. Can't they see –?'

'You think too much, that's your problem. You don't even know when you're well off, that's all I can say.'

My generation was well off. It was easy to get a job, easy to change jobs and this share clerk definitely wanted to change hers. The narrow underground tunnel walked along each morning into PT's bowels, where one bundied on, took my spirit and didn't hand it back till I bundied off each day.

I'd sit at my desk and stare into the vacant, narrow auditor's room next to me. Focus on the pattern in the bricks on the wall outside, part of the building next door. A literal brick wall. Fretted for the self who wasn't there. That self was starving. It grew thinner and thinner. Along with that self went appetite. Anxiety dried up meals. Food stuck to the palette. Even two hot meals a day, one at the canteen and one at home, couldn't put on weight.

At one stage, there seemed to be a solution. When washing hands in the washroom during tea break, one of the married women complained. 'This pill has put so much weight on.' She patted her fuller hips.

'Don't I know it,' someone else groaned.

'I need to put on weight. What's it called?'

'The contraceptive pill.'

'Where do I get it?'

They laughed. 'From a doctor but you're not married so you can't get it.'

'Why not?'

The women looked at each other. 'Are you going to tell her?'

'Not me,' the other said chuckling as she left the washroom.

'It stops you falling pregnant.' And she went on to explain.

It was not long after this that my sixteen-year-old clerk asked me about the Pill. I must have sounded quite worldly because a few days later she sat at my desk in tears.

'Are you OK?'

'I think we went too far. How do you know? What if I'm pregnant?'

'I'm not the best person to ask.'

'I'm not telling anyone else.'

'I know someone if you're okay with that. She won't tell anyone.'

'Haven't you –?'

I shook my head.

'What? Never?'

I blushed.

'Are you serious?' She mock-dropped her jaw, looked at me sideways. 'I don't believe you.'

At least I made her smile. I introduced her to my newly married contraceptive-pill friend.

That night I asked Ruby, 'How do you know when you've, you know, gone too far?'

'Oh, you'll know. Mark my word, you'll know. Let's leave it at that.'

Such was my sex education.

23

Girl Space

1963. The males in the office were always polite and friendly. The married ones constantly spoke about their wives, their children and dreams for the family. Sometimes, they asked for suggestions about where to take the wife for a special night out on her birthday or their wedding anniversary. They spoke about practical things, such as how to cut rust out of a car, how to deal with saltwater corrosion on windowsills should one live too close to the beach.

But there was a new young man in the department. He liked to walk past young women desert boot quiet. Desert Boots like to flick papers too close to breasts for our liking. He much preferred standing in our Girl Space than his own.

One afternoon, I was working at the cabinet outside the main strong room. Suddenly Desert Boots was behind me. It was difficult to turn around because he was standing too close. He leant over my shoulder, tried blowing down my neck and, at the same time, pretended to flick my bottom, but it was more of a stroke.

'If you don't mind.'

He laughed. 'Shhh.'

'How dare you!'

'Sssssh.'

'I won't shoosh.'

My mother always said, 'If someone bullies you, draw attention to them quickly, loudly. Embarrass them. They won't like it.' This technique always worked at school but I never thought I'd use it in the office.

The more Desert Boots shooshed me, the louder I got. 'Don't ever touch me like that again.'

Colleagues turned their heads and anger turned Desert Boots' face red.

The whites of his eyes glared when he lent forward and mouthed, 'Shut up. You're making a fool of yourself.'

Louder still. 'Don't tell me to shut up and I don't care if I'm making a fool of myself.' Of course, I cared. Couldn't stop trembling from his invasion of Girl Space but also from the urgent need to respond.

By this time, the assistant boss indicated to come into the strongroom and tell my side of the story.

Desert Boots was called in to give his side. He smiled at me, innocence oozing. 'I thought you were B.'

'You knew it was me.'

'My apologies. Sorry.' He mock-bowed.

'Well,' Mr M said, 'in future, keep your hands to yourself. You should know better.'

When I walked back to my desk, I felt as if it was my fault. Had I made too much of it? Was I being a prude?

'You did the right thing,' Ruby said. 'You nipped it in the bud. If you hadn't done that, it would only get worse. You watch, he won't come near you now.'

That had certainly been true of other bullies.

It's the end of the next working day. As we pack our trays away in Securities' strong room, I notice how slow Desert Boots packs his trays. By now, most of the big bosses are in their offices working out of sight. I hover, hoping Desert Boots will leave before me. I don't want to be in the same lift as him. He's made me feel uncomfortable all day. Occasionally he'd look across at me and smirk.

Next thing, he's holding out some trays and putting them on my desk. 'I found these. They might belong to Dividends.'

They do. Someone's forgotten to put them away.

'You know what to do with them. I don't.' He walks back to his desk.

I take the trays into the small Dividends strong room. My thoughts are Desert Boots is trying to make amends but when I turn round he's inside the strong room closing the door.

He blocks me as I try to pass. 'It's soundproof. No one will hear you.' He smirks and comes closer.

All I can smell is pipe tobacco. The veins in his neck are swollen.

'Don't. You. Ever. Do. That. To. Me. Again.' As he speaks, froth stretches like chewing gum between his lips.

I've never seen anything like it.

In Desert Boots' eyes, I'm the one at fault. A thousand things run through my mind. First priority. Survival. I hear my mother's voice, 'If you ever find yourself in a dangerous situation, remember they're probably as scared as you.'

I see his white shirt sticking to his broad, hairy chest. Stay calm. Talk down the situation. 'I'm sorry I embarrassed you.'

'You women are all the same.' He was upset about a recent broken engagement.

'I know you've had an awful time.'

'Never. Do. That. Again.'

I want to say as long as you promise not to do what you did again. 'I promise. I promise.'

'And you won't be telling anyone about this. Got that?'

'Yes. You'd better unlock the door before Mr M comes. He's due any minute to put his trays away and lock up.' That snaps the bullishness out of his fantasy.

He quickly opens the door and stands back. 'After you.' He smirks as he hurries to his desk, pulls on his checked woollen jacket with its leather elbow patches and tosses his curly head high and strides towards the lift.

I sit at my desk and shake. At least I'm out. But how did that happen? And so quickly? There's no one in Securities now. I watch for Desert Boots. What if he comes back round the corner? What will I do? What if he's waiting by the lift in the isolated stairwell? It's the only way out.

Mr H, Securities Department head, usually works back. I hurry to his office. Hope he's still there. Shaking uncontrollably now. Tears are welling in my throat to the point of hurt-burst.

'Excuse me.'

Mr H glances up and looks surprised when I walk into his office uninvited and close the door. He's on the phone. I sit down in a chair opposite him, mouthing sorry-sorry. Can't stop shaking. Mr H tells the caller he'll ring back.

'H-h-he locked me in the safe.'

Mr H walks around and pats me on the shoulder. 'I don't know what's going on here. I'll get you a cup of tea. Wait here, my dear.'

The tea ladies had left hours ago. Even so, Mr H comes back with a milky cup of hot tea, two sweet biscuits and dollops of kindness.

'Drink your tea, my dear, while I put these few things away, then we can talk.'

I want to cry into my tea.

'Now you tell me what's happened.'

'Did Mr M tell you what happened yesterday?'

He nods.

'I know I made a big fuss but, today, some of them are saying he's done it to them, too.'

Mr H is your father-away-from-home type. He's the proud father of daughters. He takes notes then sits back. 'I'm very sorry this happened, my dear. I'll speak to that young man first thing in the morning. Take tomorrow off if you like. Whatever time you need. It's up to you. He should know better. When you've collected your things, I'll take you out the front way.'

The front lift is for executives and clients only. We catch the lift and walk down the front steps. Mr H stands on the footpath and watches me until I disappear into the late afternoon ant rush.

Ruby thought it best to go to work the next day. It'd show no fear.

Mr W, whose desk was in front of mine, swivelled his chair round for our usual good morning chat. He cleaned his pipe then stoked it, ready for a new day. 'Terrible business, terrible. You'll be all right, my dear. You come to me if he tries anything. I've told my girls to speak up. So sorry, dear, but you'll be all right. We're onto him.'

D, who sat behind me, said, 'Grrrr, I'd punch him in the choppers if I could get away with it.'

Desert Boots appeared from around the corner accompanied by Mr H. He got his things. Mr W stood up immediately and blocked any view of my desk.

Mr M walked out of the strong room and said, 'Ready?'

It was the talk of the washroom, cloakroom, the hallways, the lift. So embarrassing.

On Desert Boots' return a few days later, he was quiet, polite and respected Girl Spaces. He was still working there when I left; had turned into quite the gentleman, which is not surprising considering the integrity of his mentors. All females on the third floor were grateful to those honourable, caring colleagues who so nobly supported us.

Anne, 1963, eve of 19th birthday, Sydney Town Hall Debutantes Ball.

24
Kadinsky

After bundying off at work and walking into the late-afternoon light, there was a surprise waiting by the kerbside. My now-you-see-me-now-you-don't friend was standing there, on his way to lectures, and wondered if I'd like to come.

We sat there in a physics lecture with pen and paper, the share clerk pretending to be a student. The beauty of the lines drawn on the board sang: Kadinsky, Mathematics, Music. My spirit soared with the drawings. Oh, to be in such an atmosphere. It was difficult to explain to my friend what had just happened.

We cupped palms and walked to the Roundhouse. The student headed off to a tutorial while an inspired self waited in the Roundhouse, absorbing the buzz.

Even though the psychology correspondence course was interesting, it wasn't enough. It was nothing like this. One of the new red telephones hung on the wall.

'Hi, Mum. I'm out at NSW Uni. I'll be home a bit late.'

'You're where? I suppose its because of you-know-who. Can't he leave you alone?'

'I wanted to come, OK.'

'Hmpph. You should know better by now.'

Ruby's words always made me feel shameful, but about what? The relationship wasn't anything like she indicated.

'Thanks for letting me know. I'll put your dinner on the stove.'

I couldn't seem to communicate the aloneness of spirit to anyone but did know that, whenever my friend appeared, my spirit flapped its wings and flew over to him. At this stage, where to fit? There was a world here, a uni world. My assumption was it could never be accessed by the likes of me. On the surface, I was all quack-quack-quack but below the surface I was working hard to keep myself afloat, and, for the first time ever, I envied my friend.

Eddie – educated surfie.

25
IBM Was in Town

When talking to my immediate boss, there was mention that I was looking for another job. Without my knowledge, he spoke to Mr H, who came to my desk soon afterwards and said to be at his office by 2.30. He'd arranged for me to see the company secretary.

We walked into an office with the largest polished desk, which commanded the centre of a very large room. Which secretary would have a room as large as this? Soon the secretary walked in, in a pinstriped suit. A man as a secretary?

'You see, my dear, you've gone as far as you can go but is there anything in particular you –?'

'I was wondering if I could train as an assistant trust officer.' One of the young men who'd started on the same day as me was in training. He enjoyed helping clients.

The secretary tilted his head. 'You see, we only have male trust officers but soon there'll be training for computers, a new field. Would you be interested?'

Colleagues looked sideways at computers. They were going to ignore them because they were considered a fad; no future in them. We were told there'd be jobs in the future that we couldn't imagine. In spite of the general scepticism, the introductory course would, at least, be something new to learn.

It was 1964. IBM was in town. Its new building stood at the southern end of the Harbour Bridge. It was a unique building in design when compared to its contemporary, the AMP, built in 1962. I knew some netballers who worked in the AMP building with its magnificent harbour views but they said it was like working in a sauna because the glass walls made some offices almost uninhabitable, whereas the more contemporary IBM building wore sensible sunglasses – that is, concrete sun-hoods on every floor. It was the future and it was giving us a sleek, symbolic peek.

At the same time, the hopeful sails of the Opera House were full of intriguing, undergarment geometry. It would take years of futuristic engineering before those glorious, ceramic sails caught the wind and sailed into history in 1972.

A large section of the second floor at PT had been transformed into a cool, air-conditioned room with huge banks of computers. Those of us fortunate enough to have done the introductory course felt privileged to be stepping inside the dedicated, space-like, highly secured area.

It's the end of the course. We're to be given a small exercise: a punchcard with a glitch. Identify the glitch and provide the solution. It took me back to sixth grade when we used spend whole lunch hours trying to break one another's codes. They said if we showed an aptitude for this work then we'd be assisted in further computing programming studies. The computer area is unlocked. We walk in as if into a sanctuary. Pull on white gloves. Punchcards are handed out to everyone except two of us.

'Excuse me, we don't have a punchcard.'

'That's right. You girls will type data.'

'I can't type.'

Someone laughs. 'All girls type.'

I laugh at their assumption and ask the instructor, 'Can we have a go, anyway, just for fun?'

'Sorry, girls. There are rules.'

'Because we're girls?'

At high school, we'd been told we could achieve anything we wanted, whatever we set our minds to, but it wasn't true. Why were benchmarks for women set so low?

26

Amazing Love

I thought of becoming a missionary. Corrie Ten Boom's writings were inspiring. I inhaled her book *Amazing Love*, and read and reread Amy Carmichael's books. These women were good souls who found purpose in the greater good. Maybe, waiting in the wings for me, was a missionary call. I was certainly full of it, wanting to be just like them.

Poems were scripture of another kind. Judith Wright's poems thrilled me. The way she challenged assumptions, institutions and man-made wisdoms through metaphor and symbol inspired and touched me in a way quite similar to Scriptures; church of another kind, her poems another form of worship. This eclectic reading programme began to enrich my interpretation of the Scriptures, which, until recently, had not involved any independent study. I was yet to test dogma and doctrine. This child of Christ was fearful of tainting faith with false prophets.

At the awkward age of thirteen, I'd learnt the Articles of Faith in confirmation classes and had accepted Christ as my Saviour just days before my fourteenth birthday, which was a few days before confirmation; knelt there in awe of Christ's sacrifice for mankind; in awe of His life, His teachings, values and beliefs.

Many years later. It's morning service. We're singing hymns, Psalms, kneeling in silence, offering prayers. Being as one; feeding soul, soul, soul. I fall deeper into the service. The sermon is on the Lordship of Christ. Lordship hurtles me through space. Spirit soars. There's consciousness of a world within; a vastness of eternity within. It's the universe, energy, love. Me. This is it. This is it. This is the scheme of things. Love. Overwhelming love. Infinite love. It's up to me, not my parents, not the church, not friends, not traditions, not institutions. It's my path and it's disturbing.

Uncertainty is an undesirable state in the low Evangelical church in which I sit, of which I'm part and whose worship I adore, but now I have uncertain thoughts through the Lordship of Christ. So much within; thoughts no longer aligning with dogma or doctrine; answerable to myself, to love, to the greater good. A rose is a rose is a rose.

By the end of the service, I can hardly stand. I sit as if nailed to the pew. Stuck, weighed down by love and awareness. Wait for the congregation to disperse and hurry out. I don't want this feeling disturbed.

I'm acutely aware as I walk home, in the midday sun, of the flickering, filtered light dancing at the foot of big shady trees. I'm heavy yet weightless; hold on to love, being, is; seeking true north.

On the bus to and from work, I listen to and watch the patter of chatterboxes around me as they reveal unintentional shadows in poetic, suspensive pauses. Their body language of face stimulates my imagination; I imagine their subtext but can't face my own. Yet. Can't keep travelling to and from work fearful of panic attacks, fearful of a lack of direction and purpose within.

In the bus of a morning, I sit beside a friend. We embroider afternoon tea cloths. The bus whisks us through Crows Nest, down the hill to North Sydney and across the Harbour Bridge. Each stitch anchors me. The pull of the long, double-stranded thread stops me from fraying. Fine needlework captures the beauty of truth in line and colour and each meditative stitch eclipses the bleak trip.

Distress catches up with me as I walk the last few hundred yards to work along the chilly city street. My surroundings take on a surreality. It's as if I'm hovering above, looking down on myself walking, talking, caught in the morning, peak-hour rush. Super-consciousness comes up and stands beside me. It reminds me how timelessness gives birth to every eternal moment, every action. When I buy my regular pineapple and lime crush from the lady, there are internal questions. Does she want to be here? Is she living her dream? If not, how does she cope? My eyes search hers for clues.

27
Who'd Want to Marry Her?

I'm halfway through the correspondence course. Maybe it can be used to find work which involves the study of people and their behaviour? Maybe I can research this frightening, awesome world of which I'm a part, a minuscule cell. What's my purpose? What's my meaning?

It was very much office culture to wait for Mr Right to charge in on his white horse, fall in love with him, get engaged, marry and raise a happy family. It always concerned me just how easily a relationship slipped into marriage, from which, Ruby always pointed out, there was no turning back.

Usually office gossip in the cloakroom was about someone's engagement, wedding plans or an unexpected break-up. One morning it was all about the secretary downstairs. She was leaving. She wasn't getting married or going overseas. She was going to be a teacher. She'd been accepted into teachers' college, where she could study at night and be a student teacher during the day. The gossip centred around her age. Everyone was aghast. She was twenty-one and she'd be studying for years. Talk was that she'd be really old before she finished. She was crazy. Who'd want to marry her then? I flew downstairs. Quizzed her. What? How? Where? When? She gave me the name of the Teachers' Guild of New South Wales.

That week, in confidence, I spoke to my friend's mother, Mrs M. There was a lot to consider. Mr and Mrs M understood my dilemma and helped fill out the application. I met all criteria. I understood that if accepted I'd work as a student teacher in an independent school. Entry to the course was competitive. It had a quota. There were no scholarships and it would mean three years of fees.

I'd never withheld important information from my parents

before but knew that this decision would meet with resistance. After the interview, and after an offer of a place in the next year's intake, I announced my intention.

'We can't afford this,' Ruby said.

'I'll pay my way.'

'You'll only get a fraction of what you get now.'

'I'll be right.'

'You'll have to pay the same board.'

'Mu-u-m...'

'I'm sorry but that's how it is.'

'I'll get a Saturday job if I have to, even if I go back to Grace Bros.'

My unexpected change in direction unsettled Ruby. She was like a lion circling her cub. Usually I was an open book but not in this instance. I didn't record it in my journal, as was my wont. I instinctively knew to leave out any musings about it.

I'd been keeping a journal of sorts, inspired by spiritual mentors: Augustine, Carmichael, Ten Boom. I'd suspected for some time now that my journal was not entirely private, so, in this instance, Ruby had no forewarning and, therefore, little influence. This decision would displease her but I needed to be strong in my stand.

When I told my parents the course couldn't be started until there was a vacancy in the independent system, which would, hopefully, lead to a teaching position, Ruby thought that was highly unlikely. Part of me thought so too, but getting this far was, surely, a sign.

After posting some letters, I was interviewed and offered the position of student teacher at Ascham Infants' School in the eastern suburbs of Sydney. I'd receive a monthly student's wage.

*

'...from ego to soul...
spirit has to be freed with persistence and imagination...
over a long period of time'

Thomas Moore

28
Last Chance

When the Banker heard my plans, he, too, was upset. His reaction was as expected. 'Why would you want to choose teaching over marriage?'

We'd been going out in a light-hearted, non-steady fashion for about a year. When I told him I was leaving work to go teaching, he couldn't see why I'd tie myself down to study when, at twenty, I could be getting engaged, married and having babies.

'I can't marry a teacher.' He stood back as if I was contagious. 'I can't marry a teacher.' Chewed on his nails. 'I won't.'

'I'll still be the same person…start February next year.'

My colleagues at work kept any criticisms to themselves. At my farewell, they gave me a beautiful brown leather briefcase with the monogram CAB. They, I, couldn't have been more proud of this generous gift. On the way home in the bus, I hugged my shiny new briefcase, intoxicated by the scrumptious smell of new leather. The briefcase overflowed with chocolates and good wishes. I'd miss my lovely workmates but as we crossed the bridge the late-afternoon glow on the harbour, with its turquoise blue lustre, stirred within me a fluttering.

The Banker persisted. He insisted I give up this silly idea. He had investments. Marriage was important. He was already on the right career trajectory. I'd be a capable, hospitable wife and a stable homemaker. These were the next criteria to be met on the rungs of his corporate ladder.

At one stage in the relationship, there was indirect pressure for me to commit and, on a whim, one Sunday afternoon, he took me home to meet his parents. Fortuitously, they were out. We walked down a narrow hallway into a living room which was overflowing with artificial flowers, the latest fad in interior decorating. We stood in the darkened living room and he hugged me tight. I could see that he admired the double-sponge-strawberry-jam-and-cream home his mother had made. He was showing me his dream.

It was revealed in those jumbo-sized yellow and pink plastic roses. It was as if my lungs collapsed. All affection, whatever it was I felt for him, sucked right out of me. I resisted the urge to run but said something about having commitments elsewhere. Needed air. Should've been honest with him but wasn't because it was obvious he adored his mother and he looked so proud of her handiwork. Should've warned him. It was inconceivable to think of me, spending hours, dusting floral delusions for anyone.

Hurrying out the front door and into the fresh air made me feel ashamed. His mother's loving domestic handiwork was something of which he was proud. But it was the plastic roses. They didn't need water or light to survive.

One evening, a few weeks later, in the first term of my course, I had a visitor who arrived with an ultimatum. 'This is your last chance.' The Banker was an affectionate, generous soul and very persistent. He was always giving me one last chance. It didn't help his cause to arrive inebriated.

The inebriated one lumbered towards the kitchen, where Stan and Ruby were trying to look inconspicuous. During his rambling discourse, I remained seated on the rug in the living room.

'Mrs B, can't you make her see sense?'

Oh, if only he knew how hard she'd tried. This was the same daughter she'd reprimanded over the years for passing up so many nice young men. Ruby assumed I'd settle down soon, marry and have a gentle, loving relationship like she and Stan. That was the expectation.

But what always worried me regarding marriage were the simplistic statements offered in regard to such a complex issue. Where were the allowances for the what-ifs? 'Mum, when two people come together, I mean, how can you be so certain?'

'You'll understand one day. Mr Right is out there, you mark my word, but at the rate you're going no one will ever be good enough.'

My visitor waved his arms pointing to the books on the rug. 'It's them or me.'

Everyone looked at me. He already had Ruby's approval and Stan's sympathy. 'If you don't – books – I –'

Stan pointed to the teapot. 'Need another drink, mate?'

'There's no getting through to her.'

Stan poured him a strong black. 'Got to admit you're on a lost cause there.'

The Banker sat down with Stan and explained how he had a very good job. One day he'd be a bank manager. He was offering Stan's daughter a very good life. And this offer would be for the very last time. 'Going, going, g…'

The men stood and shook hands. Ruby patted him on the back. I walked him to the front door, wished him well and felt relief when he stumbled away, disgusted with me and not wanting a goodnight kiss. While I didn't want to be cruel to this harmless, charming, young man I knew we were heading in different directions. I'd found my true north.

Soon there was news. He'd found a suitable partner. Within a couple of years, he married, became an assistant bank manager and father of twins and I'd almost finished my course.

29

'I Saw Tomorrow –'

As a student teacher at Hillingdon, Ascham, I smiled as I carried in heavy crates of milk left at the Infants' back door. I smiled at myself smiling as I stood at laundry tubs and scrubbed Kindergarten paint trays, day after day, in a chilly wind.

It was bliss sitting on the grass of an afternoon with my own little class exploring concepts of number. We'd gather one then two then three stones; one, two, three leaves. I never expected that exploring concept of number could be so exciting. Children squealed with understanding. These squeals were seeds sprouting. The children's enthusiasm instilled in me an enduring, lifelong love of teaching, sharing, empowering.

That first year, 1965, I occasionally sent a smile to my friends at P.T. If they could've seen me
– sitting at the breakfast table desperately trying to keep my eyes open,
– walking down the steep hill to the bus stop, only managing to open one eye,
– shivering at the bus stop on a chilly winter's morning,
– waiting for the 7 a.m. 273 bus, struggling to carry bulging briefcase, up the steep narrow stairs of the double-decker bus, to the front seat,
– attempting to decipher indecipherable handwritten lecture notes from the previous night,
– cleaning up vomit in the children's washroom,
they'd have thought me crazy.

And I was, happily, crazily in love with life and work. No more panic attacks. No more anxiety. Sheer bliss held up the weight of exhaustion.

Money-wise, everything worked out really well. Extra money came in unexpected ways. I was asked to tutor a primary school student in maths, twice a week. That helped pay board and fees.

Third year of college, we had a few lectures but our main task was to write a fifteen-thousand-word thesis on, quote, something like 'I saw tomorrow looking at me through young children's eyes and I thought…' By this time, I had a demanding, but inspirational, full-time teaching position at Abbotsleigh Junior School on Sydney's North Shore. The mistress-in-charge was on the board of the Teachers' Guild of NSW and, one day, she asked me if I'd stay back. She needed to talk.

Miss R ushered me into her office and closed the door. She shuffled papers on her desk and was a riper shade of peach than usual. 'I have some questions to ask you about your thesis. The questions are set by the board. I'll need you to answer them as best you can. I'll take notes and report your answers back to them.'

This all sounded very serious but I assumed every student would be undergoing the same procedure. Questions centred on certain extracts. I was to explain them in my own words. I thought it self-explanatory but did my best to elaborate and put it into context in the overall thrust of the thesis.

Miss R sat back and sighed. 'I had to ask you these questions because some members of the board doubt you've written this thesis yourself.'

I was incredulous. I'd lived my thesis almost to the exclusion of all else, except for teaching, which complemented what I was researching and writing. 'If they're unsure, would it be better if I spoke to them?'

'One last question. Did anyone help you write it, like a ghostwriter?'

'I'm not too sure what you mean.' I'd never heard the expression.

'It's where someone helps you write it.'

'No.'

Although, in a way, my father did. He was my listening post. He'd listen to me as I whispered in the middle of the night. He'd listen to its theories and predictions. It was probably more accurate to say that I was my own ghostwriter because of ghostlike appearances at my parents' bedroom door at midnight or in the early hours of the morning. I'd look in to see if there was a tiny red glow on Stan's cigarette. If there was, I'd creep in, go around and sit in his chair by the bed and whisper, 'Do you mind?'

He'd switch on the lamp. 'Fire away.'

Years later, Stan reckoned he should've been given a diploma too. 'Cripes. You'd come in and annoy your old man. I'd have to listen to some highfalutin' idea at two in the morning.'

I used to tape my work over and over. I'd listen to it when I drove to and from school, up and down the Pacific Highway. I put the tape recorder on the passenger seat beside me and put a notepad on my knee. As I drove, I'd listen to the flow, listen for inconsistencies of thought or example and jot down any corrections or additions that needed to be made. To date, it was one of the most blissful experiences of my life. I had no idea it was called Writing.

The mistress-in-charge said she'd provide the board with a written report. Thankfully it was unanimously accepted and I was awarded a High Distinction for my thesis. It wasn't the first time, and wouldn't be the last, that someone in authority would raise doubts about the original source of my written word.

One of the board, a well-known principal, but unknown to me, was considered a progressive educator. She asked my boss if I'd mind lending her the thesis. She said she'd approached *The Australian* newspaper, I think it was, and they indicated they might publish some extracts in a series, 'The Future of Education'. Fortunately, I kept a carbon copy because I was never to see my original bound thesis again although I often asked for its return. I never heard of any extracts being published either.

INDEX.

	Page:
Part I.	
1. The Changing Pathway of Life	1 - 3
2. Its Passport	4 - 6
3. The Growth of Education	7 - 9
4. Education is Influenced By Its Relatives: Society, Economy, Ability, Equality.	10 - 13
5. Responsibilities	14 - 18
6. Education for Living	19 - 26
7. The "Whole" Child	27 - 30

Part II.	
1. The Profession	31 - 33
2. Its Responsibilities	34 - 36
3. Harmony of the Two	37 - 40

To imagine one's self as the writer, having his thoughts (how we imagine them to be), was a most challenging situation!

Where was the starting point? What did he see looking at tomorrow, through young children's eyes?

Many viewpoints could have been discussed, but it was essen to keep one main theme in view and relate all else to it, for rea clear to us all.

After much research and discussion, there was eventually no in my mind as to what the theme should be.

Education: As it will be the child's passport while travel life's journey throughout tomorrow's world.

C. A. Ruth.

30
Thanks, Dad

I finally sat for my licence in 1965. It was during the July school holidays and until then I drove only when we were on family annual holidays so Stan and I could share the driving. But, these days, I needed a car. The books were too heavy to carry to and from school, and to and from lectures in trains and buses. Somehow, I managed to squirrel enough money away to save for a deposit on a car early in my second year of college. I bought a retired, faded, grey Austin A30, BHE (Butt's Hot Eagle). It had passed its use-by date, which is why it was so cheap.

Although I was quite confident when driving, Stan still took me on some very difficult routes before I sat for the driving test. My brother, Robert, drove me to Mosman Police Station. Because it was winter school holidays, I wore jeans, a big sloppy jumper, headband and court shoes.

The test was nowhere near as difficult as the ones my father put me through.

After the test, I parked outside the police station and the instructor said, 'You need more experience.'

Inside the station, he opened his diary and said something like, 'We'll make an appointment for next week.

'What did you say the problem was? Why did I fail?'

'You need more experience.'

'But how can I get more experience in a week?'

'Of course you can.'

It made no sense.

'I won't be able to come back next week. I'll be back at work.'

Abbotsleigh JuniorSchool.

He harrumphed. 'You mean at school.'

So that was it. He thought I was a schoolgirl. It was common practice, in those days, to fail the younger ones on their first attempt. At this stage, I was only weeks away from turning twenty-one. I had his measure now.

'Well, in a way, I'll be back at school. I teach at a school in the eastern suburbs and study at night so I won't be able to come during the day. Could I please have another appointment in the next day or two? Would that be possible?'

He stared, or was it glared, at me. He made another appointment but said it wouldn't be with him because he couldn't fit me in.

The next driving test was two days later and on the same day I had a job interview. This time I was dressed in interview mode; tailored matching jacket and skirt, pearls, high heels; definitely no jeans, sloppy jumper or headband in sight.

Stan drove me down and a different instructor took me out for my test unaware I'd already sat for it a couple of days earlier. Towards the end of the test, we stopped on a steep hill, one of the many that head down towards Balmoral Beach. I was instructed to reverse park between two cars, which I did quite comfortably.

'Who taught you to drive?'

'My father.'

'Well, tell him from me, will you, that he's done a bloody good job.'

My job interview was with the refreshing and formidable Betty Archdale, principal of Abbotsleigh, Wahroonga. Currently, I was working at the brilliant Hillingdon Infants, Ascham, Edgecliff. But, because I was studying primary and not infants, I needed to change departments for the second year of my course.

At the end of a successful interview, we stood and shook hands. Ms Archdale walked me to the front gate and pointed out the safest place to turn round – an impossibility on the Pacific Highway today. She waited and waved as I drove south but was really heading true north.

Kindergarten students and Anne at 'Hillingdon', Ascham, Edgecliff.

31
Hazelbrook

At the ripe old age of twenty-three, considered 'over the hill' by some, I bought a block of land. My overseas travelling money was accruing in the bank a goodly sum, also enough to put down a deposit. I was interested in two blocks. One was in Arterial Road, St Ives, and the other in Hazelbrook, Blue Mountains.

The mountain block was advertised as reclaimed land and was within budget. I knew the area well. It was in the former sanatorium grounds, just around the corner from where Nanna and Aunty used to live. The block in St Ives was also familiar territory. It was just up the hill from where we used to go for family picnics down by the creek. We'd sit on clear, white sand by the creek's edge. We'd scribble in the sand and slither stones along the smooth, narrow ribbon of blue silk.

The St Ives block was mostly rock.

Stan said, 'I don't know about this one, Twerpo.'

Ruby said, 'It's not a very practical block. You'd have to build too close to the road.'

I agreed but before leaving stood on the highest peak of rock and spread my arms wide and delivered a six-point sermon. 'Build. Your. House. Upon. The. Rock.'

Ruby said, 'Come down before you –'

We headed for the mountains to the block that was really calling me. In the back of my mind, I dreamt of building an A-frame split-level on a mountain bush block. Hopefully, I could teach at one of the local schools.

As a child, I often dreamt of going to Hazelbrook Primary. I could even see my desk. It was by the window and I looked out over an awesome mountain range and into the distance, almost back to 68 Penshurst Street. Whenever we went to the mountains, as soon as we reached Springwood, my spirit would lift. Mountain fragrance. Excitement would roar through my veins and still does today whenever I approach the foothills of the mountains.

'You know, your old man wanted to live up here but your mother wouldn't be in it.'

'Stan…'

'It's true.'

Ruby turned red and my ears flapped. Perhaps I'd overheard this as a young child. Maybe that was the reason why I'd fictionally enrolled myself at the local school. But Ruby was a city girl at heart so the block, where we walked of an afternoon, gathering bark at the foot of grandmother gums, next door to Nanna's, became known as 'Stanley's lot'.

Nanna and Aunty lived around the corner from their neighbour, Mrs Elliott, who cooked and cleaned for Dymphna Cusack and Florence James, who were also neighbours but in the opposite direction. They were busy writing *Come in Spinner*, which was published in 1951.

The story goes that while Mrs Elliott worked she told them stories about her life. They encouraged her to write it. She was a humble woman and followed their instruction.

Often when we visited Hazelbrook, Aunty and I would walk around to Mrs Elliott's and have afternoon tea. I wore irons then and was fascinated by Aunty's right foot, which faced outwards at a forty-five-degree angle. I used to try and copy her. I loved going out with Aunty. I'd climb into her bed of a chilly morning in the canvas-enclosed veranda and we'd listen to the chorus of currawongs.

To my child's mind, I remember Mrs Elliott made nice afternoon teas. I have a memory of butterfly patty cakes. They had butterfly wings, set in cream, powdered with icing sugar. I always felt so grown-up sitting there with my great-aunt and her friend, whom they liked to keep an eye on.

Both Nanna and Aunty were privy to the various stages of the autobiographical novel, *Caddie*. Cusack and James would check the writing and instruct where it needed more detail; here, there, here, there.

Nanna and Aunty worried about her. 'The poor soul. It's affecting her health.'

To the best of my memory, Mrs Elliott's writing table was in a small, closed-in veranda, just off the main living room. It overlooked a north-easterly meadow bordered by tall pines, eucalypts and Japanese maples. Mrs E had a racking cough and sipped on cough mixture throughout the day, because, as Nanna said, 'They work her to the bone. They expect far too much of her.'

Caddie was published in 1953 and was a success. Nanna and Aunty's copy of the book was passed down to Stan. Many years later, Ruby wrote inside its cover, in pencil, 'Mrs Elliott'. It was so we'd know who the author was, Nanna and Auntie's friend, the one who wished to remain anonymous. We were told not to tell anyone. As her-story goes, the novel became an Australian classic and made into a film in 1976. Mrs Elliott was no longer anonymous.

The mountain block in which I was interested sat high on a ridge. It had a steep drop at the back and in the distance was the grey-green patchwork quilt of Penrith plains. As children we'd walked this ridge many times when we collected pine cones for the open fire.

Collecting day was always a significant family outing. Thermoses and sandwiches were packed and we'd sit and rest on fallen logs in the heart of the pine forest in the sanatorium grounds. Black-green. Dark. Cool. Sacred pine-needle music. Scented cathedral. Thin rays of light.

Collecting days were a mixture of fear and fun. What if the Banksia Men were true? My head was crammed with May Gibbs's bush stories and I had a sneaking suspicion her characters were real. Old men banksia trees were everywhere. In the thick of the forest, it was best to stay close to the adults. 'Don't go running off, getting lost,' Ruby used to call out to the boys while I walked as close to her as possible. I couldn't understand how the boys could be so brave with all those Banksia Men ready to jump out and grab them.

At the end of the day, Stan would carry a full sack on his back and we'd carry baskets full of fragrant pine cones. At the end of our little holiday, Stan would always make sure that his mother and aunt had plenty of firewood before we left. As we headed back down the mountain, we looked out for steam trains and counted their engines and carriages. We also had a game as to who saw the first calliopsis, which grew profusely along the edges of the narrow Great Western Highway. They looked like golden cuffs.

On the day I bought my block of land, I found a waratah in full bloom. It was tempting to pick and take it back but I resisted. It belonged there.

Financing the block was straightforward. No responsible male was required to sign on my behalf. I put down a large deposit and paid it off as quickly as I could. Ruby rested more easily after I showed her the title deed. By now, my parents had purchased their own home in Artarmon Road, Willoughby, but Ruby always feared loans of any kind. She wanted to know what I intended to do with a block that only had kerb and guttering but no water or electricity.

I shocked my mother one afternoon when I came home from work and expressed my intention to sell land and car to fund an overseas trip. What ensued was probably the biggest argument we ever had. In summary, she said, 'You can go overseas on the condition you don't sell your land. That way you've got something to come back to.'

K, my travelling companion, was keen to go sooner than we'd planned. Her sister worked in the Vatican so she was keen to go as soon as possible. I felt pangs of dread at the thought of selling my land. I knew then that I preferred a bush block to a gangplank.

32

The Novocastrian

He was a proud Novacastrian (N). He boarded somewhere west of Parramatta and taught economics and geography at a very tough high school. He seemed unfazed by the real and imagined threats from parents should he try to discipline their children. At the same time, I was teaching privileged primary students and was amazed he kept returning to work each day. I felt sure I couldn't have done that under such volatile conditions.

N was reserved and droll with a sharp intelligence and an attractive brooding pose. His dark hair and healthy tan, along with fine, high cheekbones and shy tilt of the head, gave him a handsome aloofness. Although I was only a few centimetres shorter than him, he appeared to look at me from a great height.

I met him at North Sydney Police Boys' Club. It was one night towards the end of my first year of studies.

My girlfriends had warned me that if I didn't come willingly, they'd physically drag me away from my books. 'You haven't been out for months. C'mon. For old times' sake. It'll be fun.'

The Novacastrian arrived at a time in my life when it overflowed. Life was fruitful. I was involved in study, work, leadership training, youth camps, beach mission. There was little or no time for a relationship. Even so, N would ring midweek. I could set my clock by him. His dry sense of humour and rock-solid demeanour always won me over. He was comfy in his own skin, comfy enough to leave me to my studies and friends. There was no doubt in Ruby's mind that he was a lovely young man; a good match.

Most Friday nights after I arrived home from lectures, he'd drive across town and stay for a couple of hours. He'd stand between the kitchen and the living room, holding his suit coat over one shoulder, oh-so-casual Dean Martin style, leaning up against one of the double doors instead of Martin's grand piano and without the signature cigarette, and he'd watch me eat my reheated dinner. When he left, he mostly headed back to Newcastle for the weekend. He boarded four or five nights a week and didn't enjoy his landlady's cooking or company.

I don't ever remember us going on social outings or to shows other than the occasional dance, but we might've. Sometimes we went for a drive to see lights on water. I had an aversion to 'parking' because of the Bogle-Chandler mystery. They were lovers who died in a place called Lovers' Lane, in Lane Cove National Park, only a few miles from our place.

Rather than sit in the car, I much preferred walking, talking, paddling under starlight, digging toes into cool sand, chasing the tide, hand in hand. Better still, leaping, *Wizard of Oz* style, singing into the velvet night, 'I'm off to see the wizard…' It was not something I expected my more serious companion to enjoy.

I've always loved a sense of the ridiculous. It's my spirit level; my life balance. R didn't share the same spirit, in that way, but I admired the respectful way he handled my faith, a faith he didn't share. He suspected I was a missionary when he saw the library of Christian literature on the back seat of the car. He made it quite clear he would not be converted.

I laughed. I'd been through this before. My studies were widening my horizons but because I loved my Lord and had seen the power of prayer at work on beach missions, youth camps and in people's lives, I was not about to water down my active faith for anyone, although I was increasingly conflicted with Sydney Low Church Anglican teachings and hierarchy.

It was a personal struggle to do with interpretation and context: literal, mythological, metaphorical, symbolic, metaphysical. The church's negativity and so-called wisdom, in regard to women and their supposed unsuitability to the priesthood, limited their talent pool by fifty per cent. It was a discussion I had with my journal where inner thoughts lay bare. I should've given my journal a name because it was one of my best friends. It told me things about myself that nobody else could or would.

One night, a surprise visit by my part-time friend created a slight drama unbeknownst to him, offstage, in the family wings. It was a Sunday night and I'd been away for a girls' weekend at a guest house in Katoomba. A broken-hearted friend needed serious mollycoddling. She was recovering from the collapse of a five-year courtship. They'd been engaged for years and were only weeks away from the wedding when her fiancé told her he'd met someone else.

We took F away. We went horse riding and bushwalking. The broken-hearted soul shed tears during the main course, which was the idea, and then we had laughter and dancing for dessert. As we prepared to go home, we discovered that the trains were indefinitely delayed. One of our new found friends offered to drive us home. I had intended to invite them in for a light supper, as a way of thanking them, but when we pulled up outside 39 there was a certain white MGB.

'It looks like I have a visitor.'

Because of the eggshell nature of my relationship with the owner of the car, a relationship that was officially off, everyone was too polite to come in. It would've soon been a full house, anyway, because, at any moment, N was expected to call in on his way back from Newcastle.

When I walked into the living room, the TV was talking to itself. I saw the back of my visitor settled on a chair at one end of the kitchen table, opposite Stan. Stan, as usual, had his head buried in a crossword. E was chatting with Ruby. It seemed to be a cool reception. She sat with arms folded and looked tight-lipped. I imagined her feet would be tapping by now under the table. It was always advisable to check Ruby's feet when she was holding her tongue. At this stage, I was totally unaware that my mother had written to this fellow telling him to stay away from her daughter, telling him to let her get on with her life.

Ruby approved of N. He was lovely, quiet, a serious young man, who at least had the decency to wear proper shoes and not arrive in those wretched thongs.

On the quiet, I asked my mother to bring N through when he arrived and took my unexpected visitor into a front room. I'd recently bought a new book of poems and pointed one out to him, one that might interest him, 'The Surfer' by Judith Wright.

I didn't hear N arrive because he'd recognised the car out front and had walked around the back.

Ruby came in and said, 'Anne, you have a visitor. Eddie, it's time for you to go.'

After a goodbye hug and kiss, he reiterated, 'We can never be serious, you know.'

His aspirations and ambitions were directly in line with the rising 60s. As the aspirational class rose, my church-girl ways were more and more out of synch with rapid societal change. Alas, this young lad was never going to settle for a lass who wore a simple clerk's dark blue uniform with detachable white collar.

When we said our goodbyes, I saw N's small sedan parked right behind the white MGB. When I walked into the living room, there was a gloomy, shoulder-hunched N sitting on the lounge.

Stan broke the silence. 'Which way did you come, mate?'

'Over the bridge.'

'I hope not. Across it, more likely.'

N tried a smile. 'Across it.'

'You had me worried there for a bit.'

'I might as well have gone over it.'

Everyone looked at me.

It was school holidays and N invited me to his hometown for a weekend. No doubt, Ruby would refuse – 'No daughter of mine...' – but there was no objection, just oodles of encouragement. When, previously, E had offered to take me on a holiday to Lord Howe Island, all expenses paid, Ruby was aghast at the suggestion and made all sorts of aspersions. But with N, if he'd made a similar offer, she would, no doubt, have helped pack my bags.

Len insisted on driving me to Newcastle. He chided his mother for letting me go without finding out more. He was unsettled; wanted to check if it was kosher. We waited near Belmont, where we thought we were to meet N, but he wasn't there. We found a public phone and looked up what we hoped would be his home phone number. It was the right number but his mother knew nothing. She suggested we go back to Swansea. He might be there and he was. It appeared I was staying at his grandmother's.

Len was uncomfortable leaving, because of the mix-up, and said that if I wanted to come home, at any time, he'd come and get me. He needn't have worried; N was always respectful.

Grandmother lived in a cute cottage in a very narrow street which felt like an historic mining town's time warp. She was warm and welcoming and as non-intrusive as the street in which she lived with a back garden full of thriving plants.

N and his grandmother had a few quiet asides; behind the scenes family dynamics. He drove me around the beautiful shores of Newcastle, near where he lived, and we had dinner with his family. I knew the city beaches of Newcastle quite well having attended professional development courses during school holidays at the teachers' college in Hamilton and stayed at the YWCA opposite the college. Rather than eat in, I'd go to the little shop opposite Bar Beach and buy fish and chips and drive around the beaches, following the shoreline, and discovered a warm hug of a park, King Edward.

On our home journey, it rained so hard that the windscreen wipers worked overtime. N kept turning them off when the rain eased.

'Can you see?'

'If you leave them on, they wear out.'

'I'll buy you a new set if these ones wear out.' It was just that I liked to see where I was going, even if it cost me.

Quite soon after the weekend, N rang and mentioned that he'd wait for me to finish my course. I took immediate flight from his certainty and presumption. We hardly knew each other. Besides, I was only halfway through my course. Then, maybe, I'd teach overseas for a year or two and wouldn't want, or expect, anyone to wait for me.

So, during a seemingly uneventful midweek phone call, I made a mountain out of a molehill. By the end of the call, we'd ended the relationship.

Ruby was speechless. 'Is he all right or don't you care? That poor man.'

'Mum, we hardly know each other. I don't know his friends. He doesn't know mine.'

Years later there was news that N married. I was delighted to hear that this gentle hunk, whose wide brown eyes smouldered when he spoke, had found his match.

Bar Beach, Newcastle, 1960s.

33
Philip Baxter

It was 1966, near the end of my second year in a three-year Diploma of Primary Education, working full-time and attending lectures at night, when E rang to say he'd left teaching to study full-time. He was living in at Philip Baxter College, a residential college at the University of NSW. He mentioned that he was 'off road' for the time being. I visited him a few times. He was writing poems and read out some early ones. They had potential.

Once, I took a college assignment for him to give me his opinion. He'd sublimated his passion for painting to get a science degree. My offering was a very simple still life but it lacked something. With much *joie de vivre* the painter highlighted the capsicum and banana in a way this painter wouldn't have dared.

Whispering in his room after curfew, around 10 or 10.30 p.m., and having to sneak out without being seen, felt adolescent. One time, well after curfew, there was a knock on the door. We'd been heard. We were laughing too loud. As a result, the mature-age student had to go before a panel and face disciplinary action for having a woman in his room after hours.

We were officially in off mode so what on earth was I doing? Although neither of us was any longer as naive there were subtle changes in him which spoke of a greater worldliness to which I wasn't attuned. I climbed into the car an agitated vegemite, reprimanded myself – to think I could've been home having a long bath, instead of here, driving home, across town, alone, late at night. That was something usually to be avoided.

No sooner had the student prince waved goodbye than a station wagon full of hoons drove up beside me. It was late, well past any Philip Baxter curfew, and the normally busy road was almost deserted. The hoons wheeled beside, behind, in front of me so I took a devious route to the southern approach of the Harbour Bridge and was sure they'd gone but once on the bridge they roared past, swerved in front and slowed right down. I glanced to see that every door was locked, heart beating faster than the wheels could turn.

This wasn't the first time I'd been chased. While most of our mothers didn't have licences their daughters did, and some young men still believed the road belonged to them. After my first experience, Stan had said, 'Always lock your doors. If it happens again, put your lights on high beam and keep your hand on the horn until you reach the nearest police station.' Fortunately, North Sydney police station was only a few hundred yards off the northern side of the Harbour Bridge.

Lights on high beam, hand on the horn, I drove as steadily as my shaking hands would allow. The hoons were laughing at my desperate antics. As we approached the police station, I pulled up abruptly, leapt from the car and ran inside. The hoons accelerated. I'd made a mental note of the make of the car and numberplate. In those days, it was possible to know the make of every car on the road. I remembered the first few letters of the numberplate but fear forgot the rest. The police put out a call. I rang my parents from the station and the police escorted me to Crows Nest junction. I drove home from there, head and heart pounding. Stan was waiting on the front porch in his dressing gown and Ruby was inside filling up the teapot and putting out the cups and saucers.

One night, I'm invited to visit my painter-poet-uni friend at college. Everything seems the same. We chat, laugh and, as usual, canoodle but, at some point, my body takes over. It displays a strong will of its own, as if it has never stood up for itself before. A shooting star transports us. Fortunately we both arrive safely back on planet Earth. We're surprised, breathless. It was beautiful. Something special just happened. I know not what; aware, though, that this is precarious territory. Can't risk it happening again, not under these circumstances, because the reality is, at this point in our friendship, we're heading in different directions.

About twelve months later, I rang a good friend who worked in administration at NSW uni. She sounded upset.

'Are you okay?'

'Not really. Eddie's here. I'll put him on.'

After an awkward and unexpected greeting, he told me he'd just got engaged. In an instant, I had a mental image of an attractive young Arts student, thoroughly modern and most definitely not a church girl.

'I thought you were never going to get married.'

'I was wondering how to tell you.'

'Why should that matter?'

But we both knew it mattered. It mattered. I remember saying I hoped he'd be happy; at least, I hope I had the courtesy to say so. I walked into the kitchen and told Ruby. She could've said 'I told you so' but didn't. She would've been too busy offering up silent prayers of thanksgiving. She wouldn't have to write any more letters to this fellow, about which I knew nothing at this stage.

Some months later, I was invited to a ball at Philip Baxter College. R was your storybook tall, dark and handsome type. He was good company and a great dancer. He'd finished Wool and Pastoral Studies at the same university. I expected my Philip Baxter friend to be far away, most likely in Armidale, visiting his fiancée. Dinner suits were definitely not part of his wardrobe.

As R and I walked along the narrow corridor in the college, heading for the cloakroom, I saw the back of a familiar, tall figure standing at the cloakroom counter in a dinner suit. He stood beside a dark-haired, attractive young woman.

At least, in this instance, to be foreseen was to be forearmed. When they turned round, we shared polite introductions and, according to custom, congratulated him and admired the engagement ring. Soon the popular 'Zorba the Greek' was playing and R and I were lost in dance.

34

Darwin and Central Australia

Safari, 1969. During the August/September school holidays I went on a safari camping trip around much of Australia, crossing the borders of New South Wales, Queensland, Northern Territory, South Australia and Victoria. Allow £2 per day for food, £121 for fare.

I wanted to see my own country before travelling overseas. Although I knew parts of this country, its interior was unfamiliar to me. There was an unexplained urge to know it more intimately. How could I go overseas and not know my own country? It didn't make sense.

The coaches left from the city. When we arrived at the terminus in Eddy Avenue, my travelling companion and teaching colleague and I were surprised to discover that our mistress-in-charge and her sister, a mistress-in-charge at another independent girls' school, were not only going on the same trip as us but we would be travelling in the same coach. They sat up the front. We sat down the back. During the first day's travel, K, who had a loud infectious laugh, and I, often caused our boss to turn round, frown and shake her head at us. We were staff of whom she wanted to be proud. Ladies didn't laugh out loud.

That night in Nyngan we asked the driver if we could swap coaches. Fortunately, a middle-aged couple were complaining about the noise in their coach, where there was community singing as they travelled. That sounded more like us.

The first night was so cold in our two-man tent that condensation dripped like a shower. We picked up our damp sleeping bags and pillows and headed for the laundry but it was already full. We eventually found floor space in the toilet block, which was also full of campers lying wherever they could. It was a five o'clock start in the morning.

We wiped layers of ice off our ports, which sat outside the small tent during the night. We'd sightsee throughout the day, and set up camp before dark. We rarely put up our tents. We lit a campfire each night and cooked our meals over it, talked, laughed, sang, told jokes and tall stories. Each night we'd have to blow up our air bed before climbing, exhausted, into our sleeping bags. There were few showers around and after a few days we soon took on the colour of the earth and our hair felt like straw.

One night, we slept beside a roadhouse. I'd never been to a roadhouse before. It was full of hard-working, lonely men holding up the bar. They worked on properties deep inland and had come in to spend their pay and seek company. I was no longer as shy but never enjoyed flirting so told one of the men who was standing too close to me for too long that I was a nun on holidays. I'd used that line once at a party and it surprised me how well it worked. As far as I knew, nuns didn't have holidays.

Word spread. I now felt shame. Such a fraud. Next thing, all those spiritually inclined in the roadhouse were lining up to speak while others crowded around. What to do? I told them my friend, who was standing beside me, was also a nun. K was not impressed but, at least, that way we could share the obvious respect they had for the sisters who sat and listened to life stories that were richer than gold. These men were unforgettable, big, strong nuggets. They were the country's essential scrub. Their limbs glowed the same ochre as the Simpson Desert.

The deeper inland we travelled, the more Dorothea McKellar's words 'This wide brown land,' resonated. We recited it. Here were the misty mirages which had seduced so many early explorers into sometimes tragic and false belief that water and shade were just up ahead, in the distance; a few more miles, a few more miles.

We travelled through years of drought and indifference to livestock. The coach stopped. We climbed out and stood amongst the desolation, in silence, witnesses to the score of bloated carcasses with their disconnected eyeballs. Was that really the sound of maggots feeding or was it only the sound of blowflies grazing? Not one stalk of grass stood. The cracked, parched skin peeled, split, screamed for relief. Such suffering. We were in a Drysdale. We stood as one. Heads bowed. City slickers silenced. We stood exposed to the underbelly of this wide brown land.

I'd been given a Darwin address by my friend, Lula. 'If you have any free time, go and see her, Betsy. You'll like her.' It was not so long ago that L had met B through her husband, who was a pastor, and she'd quite recently stayed with them. In the coach, another woman had the same address. She'd worked with her and was going to visit.

B's husband travelled great distances in his job while she raised the children. I've never forgotten the night I sat down at their dinner table. The pastor was away on another trip and it fascinated me how their mother coped. My parents had rarely spent a night apart. I didn't know of any woman who lived like this; like a single parent most of the time. I sat there fascinated, observing organisation and family politics.

One of the children said grace. We shared delicious food, laughter, stories then the children cleared the table, washed up, dried up and were soon off to bed with a blessing from their mother. Then it was adult time. This young mother didn't have a lot of adult time but she made up for it by studying. She told us how she was studying for a Bachelor of Arts degree by correspondence. She was joyful and enlightened and raised women's issues that we, as young women, would face in years to come.

B continued with her studies and became influential in women's studies at the University of NSW. She, along with colleagues, would be instrumental in introducing women's issues into the social work curriculum in the Faculty of Professional Studies. In time, she reached the esteemed position of associate professor but, for me, I'll always remember that inspiring young mother whose life's purpose was sown when living in that modest Darwin home, where she faced women's issues first hand while raising a young family in the diverse, but isolated, Northern Territory.

At Victoria Downs, the first rains came. Spots left impressions in layers of red dust. Polka dots. The coach stopped before the dust turned into slip. We made up camp behind a small store which only opened for a few hours every fortnight for the local Aboriginal people to buy supplies. There was a toilet block out the back.

K and I met three Aboriginal women nearby whose smiles were as broad as the land. We sat down together and scratched pictures in the damp red dust, trying to communicate with each other. It stopped raining but the coaches had to wait until the slush dust had hardened. The coach wasn't going anywhere. We'd be staying here for at least twenty-four hours.

One of the coach drivers walked over to see what we were doing. He told us to come back to camp but my new-found friend Rose and I were in the middle of a conversation. Rose broke some mulga wood off a small tree nearby and carved the shape of a porcupine. She lit a small fire then heated a thin piece of bent wire in the smouldering ash. When it was hot enough, she branded porcupine quills into the wood.

The driver walked over again. 'She'll expect you to pay.'

'That's okay.'

'Only give her a couple of bob.'

He spoke like this in front of Rose. I wanted to apologise for his rudeness but she had little English. I ignored him. I hoped she couldn't understand his words but I could see that she read his body language and tone of voice. The driver walked away.

Rose handed me the porcupine. I held it, stroked it, as if it was the Spirit between us as we sat in the damp dust. K was also chatting to the other two women. They drew in the dust too. Rose picked up the remaining wood and carved two nulla nulla sticks, branding them with similar markings to the porcupine.

By this time, the sun had moved and it was time to go back to camp. Rose and I stood and hugged each other and I didn't quite know what to do next. Should I offer to pay for these beautiful carvings like the driver said? But my gut was telling me the price was a shared spirit of being, not much different to me inviting her over for afternoon tea and making her something special likes scones with jam and cream. This was Rose's hospitality.

In spite of my instincts, and just in case I was wrong, I started to open my purse but Rose hung her head, pushed her hands towards me, indicating I put it away.

'I'm sorry,' I said.

'You my daughter,' she said.

We hugged.

'Thank you, Rose. I'll cherish these. I'll never forget you.' And I've never forgotten her generous soul or the image of her standing there, barefoot, in the damp dust, dark curly hair, bright floral dress, arms up, waving as K and I walked past their humpies and back over the slight grade and out of sight.

By the time we reached Cooper Pedy, the five-year drought had broken. We couldn't travel further south because the road was thick with slip. We'd have to wait until the graders came the next day and carved a way out. We camped well outside the town so we'd be one of the first in a long line of travellers.

We headed into town for a meal. We visited the underground opal house. The quick-tempered wind sent us back quickly to camp, earlier than planned. Half the tents were blown away or ripped apart. Amazingly, our tent was still standing so we slept in it with raincoats on in case it flew away during the night. The coach was full of sleeping campers and the graders arrived at dawn.

Meanwhile, an urgent message was passed onto us. Our mistress-in-charge was in town and had arranged to fly back with her sister because they couldn't risk being late at the start of the new term. The message indicated that it would be best for us fly back with them.

We declined the invitation. We still had days to go. We were yet to witness first hand the extravagant bounty of the rain; purple and yellow reaching the far horizon just outside Wilcannia and Broken Hill. Admittedly, we arrived in Sydney just the day before school was due back but we were still in time for staff chapel service and staff meetings.

That first night home, the ten to eleven-foot ceilings seemed low. Likewise, in the staff room next day, there seemed to be too many people, too many walls. When walking backwards and forwards along the long, narrow corridor to and from my classroom, I felt stifled and craved fresh air and open spaces.

Part of me was still out there scattered around the countryside. I was still back with Betsy and her family, with Rose and the mulga wood, with the excited camel kids, the bloated sheep, the storeys-high burnt umber anthills, the magnificent conglomerate, sacred Uluru. I was astonished by the resilience of ferns flourishing in the Olgas; at the simple blossom of Sturt's rose at Simpson's Gap and the brilliant burst of Sturt's desert pea at Pichi Richi, bursting at the foot of Rickett's sculptures. My cup was full.

'As the human evolutionary – reaching out for the higher meaning – attains the higher radiant degrees of consciousness, and still higher until we touch upon the Christ consciousness, it is then the body becomes diffused with a light, beauty and love, then we know this love to be the Divine Spring, the living waters flowing outwards upon all earth life…'

William Ricketts
Sacred earth-site – William Ricketts Sanctuary
Alice Springs, Northern Territory
'Understanding Love'

35
A Man and a Woman

When I arrived home from work one day with K, she pointed to a parked car. 'Isn't that Eddie?'

We greeted him and went inside to have afternoon tea; sat and listened. He had separated from his wife and was in Sydney for a short stay. Later that night we went to dinner.

Before he arrived to pick me up, Ruby warned of dire consequences if I went out with a married man. 'If you do, there'll be a private detective following you, you mark my words. You'll be co-respondent in the divorce courts before you know it.'

'Mum, they've separated.'

'Next thing they'll be getting a divorce. I don't believe in them. Butts don't divorce.'

While we sat at a table for two in a restaurant in King's Cross, just down from the Australian Museum, it was disconcerting when a well dressed gentleman walked in shortly after us. He sat alone at a nearby table and rested his briefcase on top of the table. He could've been cast for *Goldfinger*. He often looked our way. I can't remember what if anything I ate that night because, by now, I was convinced that the lone diner was probably the private detective Ruby had warned me about and he had a hidden camera. How many photos had he taken? Once outside in the fresh air, my thoughts reset. Any photos taken would've shown a man and a woman sitting, talking, eating. We weren't doing anything wrong.

After dinner we saw the movie *A Man and a Woman*. I enjoyed it and ensured there was no reason to be cited in an adultery case and bade the traveller well.

But a night or so later, there was a tapping on the bedroom window. I pulled back the blind. The traveller was inviting me to come back with him to Armidale for a few days during the coming school holidays. I climbed out of bed and met him at the back door, unaware that my sister thought she heard everything and had raced inside and told her mother that her sister was running away with E.

We were standing in the laundry when Ruby flung open the door. 'What on earth do you think you're doing here at this time of night?'

Once she was reassured that he was on his way back to Armidale, and her daughter wasn't going anywhere, she went inside but stood guard by the front bedroom window. Her silhouette was obvious as we said goodbyes. It was just as well she didn't see him pick me up and carry me down the driveway. She might've thought there was an abduction underway. I'm not too sure from where she would've rallied troops but, certainly, she had invisible forces at the ready. Of course I wanted to go but I couldn't accept his mistress-accepted, marriage-rejected offer.

'No fault' divorce didn't become law until years later, not until 1975. Before that if a couple separated they had to wait a couple of years to divorce. If one of the parties strayed during that time, then they could be called upon as a co-respondent. If it was a woman, her reputation would be ruined.

There was a reputation to consider. Recently, at an independent boys' school, an unmarried master and mistress were found to be residing together in the masters' quarters. The mistress was sacked. The master remained, reputation and rank intact, while hers was tarnished. She had to move overseas to start again.

If I went away with my friend, I couldn't trust myself. And, more importantly, what if his feelings were merely rebound? If he was serious, he needed to get a divorce and move back to Sydney. At the time, I didn't know anyone in my age group who'd separated, so I didn't know the process. All I knew was what I'd been told. I didn't want to be a potential co-respondent. It sounded so ugly when reported in the press. For a single woman in the late 60s, there were still so many what-ifs and buts to consider. We said our goodbyes and some of my spirit went with him.

*

Waratah

I tend with lover's touch
the sun-kissed crown of waratah
and stumble. Scarlet falls
beneath my feet and carpets deep regret's dark pain.

36

The Perfect Companion

It was a rash moment when I agreed to join the church choir. I had avoided it over the years because of a private protest. Tradition had it that girls couldn't join the choir until they turned sixteen. Boys were said to have the more pure soprano. Both my brothers had been choirboys. We were a family of singers and I longed to sing in services, especially on Saturday afternoons. The choristers had a front-line view at all those beautiful weddings and it was a way of earning an extra sixpence or two.

The minister, Rev. B, spoke to me one afternoon in the church hall when I was helping in the kitchen in preparation for our monthly fellowship tea. It was a week before my sixteenth birthday.

He walked over and said with great gusto, 'Well, my girl, you'll soon be old enough to join the choir.'

I spoke as quietly as I could. 'I don't think so.' I'd been thinking about it and was indignant about the unfairness surrounding the junior choir. I had prepared my answer should anyone ask me to join.

'Yes,' he said, 'we're looking forward to it.'

I looked him in the eye and said quietly, in a just-between-you-and-me voice, while looking up at this tall imposing reverend, who was also an army chaplain and stood like an officer. 'I think, Mr B, if I can't be in the choir today, this week or last week because I'm a girl then I don't want to be in it next week or the week after, if you know what I mean.'

Stan laughed out loud when he heard what I'd said but quickly checked himself when Ruby coloured and said, 'You what?'

'You've got a point there, Twerpo,' Dad said. 'What did the old coot have to say for himself?'

'He smiled and patted me on the shoulder, like he sort of agreed. He said to go home and think about it and he hopes I'll change my mind but he said it's up to me.'

'Good on him.' Stan liked the Reverend B.

On the other hand Ruby was still catching her breath. 'Have you no respect?'

'I just said I didn't think it was fair.'

'I never know what's going to come out of your mouth.'

'He didn't mind. I don't think it's fair that boys can join the junior choir and girls can't.'

Ruby shook her head. Her lips were stretched so tight nothing could escape. Instead she glared. It was a look I'd seen before. It said something like, where on earth did you come from, who are you or where do you get those ideas? And, like my mother, I was trying to work out who I was, too.

'I'm not joining, Mum.'

But I joined almost a decade later. By then, my private protest was no longer applicable. Young girls had been choristers for years.

This time in my life was a very settled time. I had money in the bank, a good car, owned land, loved my job and tried to adjust to the constant changes with friends getting married and/or moving away while other friends headed overseas to avoid relationships which were heading for the altar.

In 1967, after a tour of a new university, Macquarie University, which had just opened at Ryde, I considered more study. The university had recently enrolled its first year of students. I was drawn to its Education faculty. The content sounded ground-breaking and stimulating. I thought about converting my Diploma of Primary Education into a Degree in Education.

I'd become aware that when busy teaching or creating I always felt more like myself. The year spent researching and writing my thesis had been a year of bliss. It generated in me a luminescent feeling which I wasn't able to share with anyone. It felt dorky to be saying such a thing; besides, being twenty-four, my sister was already calling me 'Georgie Girl'. In everyone's mind, it was time to get down off the shelf.

During this very contented frame of mind, I joined the church choir. I loved worship and this would be a way of contributing in song. One of the tenors, Graeme, GB, was a quiet, witty, handsome, twenty-nine-year-old. His father, Jack, had recently died. Jack had worked with Stan. 'One of nature's gentleman,' Stan used to say. I'd met Graeme's parents a few years earlier when we were holidaying at Nambucca Heads. They were staying at a guest house in town. Stan and Ruby invited them to our camping spot for afternoon tea. To give them some privacy, I stayed in the tent and read a book. They said they had a son who'd be a good match because they couldn't get his head out of a book either.

Graeme sang in the choir and also in the same small singing group as my sister. They chatted easily during breaks and often some members of the choir would head back to our place for supper where the teapot was always full. One night, GB came back to 39.

As often happened, weekend arrangements were made on Thursday nights after choir. Some decided to go to the pictures on Saturday night but I didn't commit.

Graeme turned and said, 'Would you like to go?'

I wasn't going out with others these days. Still felt guilty about the Novacastrian. I never expected men to be so proactive about settling down. Weren't they always the ones who joked women chased them? I had other agendas even though there were one or two special souls I really liked.

GB had lashings of wit, slices of cynicism and a dramatic flair. He had an incredible general knowledge, was artistic, a keen photographer, and made me laugh.

Going against my intuition, I said, 'That'd be nice. Thank you.'

We'd be in a group so it wouldn't necessarily mean I was only going out with him.

GB was the perfect companion. We went to shows, dinners, pictures and outings with friends. In a way, it was just like being in the movies. And there was no pressure sexually. He seemed to be a good church boy. When we hugged, he smelt so fresh of Palmolive, and his shirts of Fabulon. And, for the first time, he was the most perfect fit for my family. This was definitely new territory. It felt so familiar it was disconcerting. Was this what Ruby meant when she said, 'Oh, you'll know Mr Right. It's different.'

Within weeks, Graeme was professing his love but I couldn't reciprocate.

'It's too soon. I can't get serious.'

We became engaged on Christmas Eve 1969. Just before our first date I'd been interviewed for a teaching position in the Southern Highlands. The job entailed moving, teaching years five and six and being mistress-in-charge of a very small junior school. I had accepted the position. I'd already given a term's notice to my current employer and was planning to move into one of the school's boarding houses at the end of January, before any boarders arrived.

When this teaching opportunity was put to me, it seemed too good to be true. It was neglectful of me not to check the staff's past history, which Mrs H, my teaching colleague, had suggested. 'I think you'll find there are problems.' It wasn't her place to tell me what she knew. An unwritten code in this staffroom was no gossip.

I tried to rescind the teaching position; explained the recent engagement. The principal said come anyway. In the meantime, she'd look for a replacement.

37
Southern Highlands

In the new year, 1970, I took up the teaching position. The school had a magical setting and so much potential. It was the realisation of a dream to teach in a small country school. The day students and boarders were delightful and unassuming in manners with wide horizons in their eyes. I would cherish this opportunity, this year, before moving back to the city and getting married. But forces within and forces without were such that twelve months was going to be unrealistic.

Stan suffered from an unusual form of emphysema and was off work more often. My sister, who still lived at home, didn't drive, nor did Ruby, so when Stan was ill there was no driver. Ruby was feeling the stress and so was I. We had much to do on weekends when I came home: weekly shopping, messages to run, medications to pick up, wedding plans to organise. Weekends were so hectic it soon became necessary to drive home midweek to help out.

Rising early next morning, with early morning mist as my companion, and with a need to focus on low flying, within speed limits, of course, I'd nibble on Mummy-made brekkie sandwiches and drink tea from the hot Thermos cup as I headed south. My eye was always on the clock because it was important to be back in time for chapel and to take junior assembly.

At twenty-five, this was the first time I'd left home. When offered live-in accommodation at the school, it seemed a sensible idea; a young woman on her own in an unknown town and it would only be for twelve months.

It didn't take long to discover there weren't enough feet on which to stand. It was common knowledge in the staffroom that the previous one or two junior school mistresses-in-charge had left due to nervous exhaustion.

Live-in conditions were basic. The bedroom was tiny, on the left, halfway up the stairs in a grand old home. It was a couple of kilometres from the main school. Apart from teaching composite five-six there were extra duties running a small junior school which had less than sixty students from kindy to year six. There were many additional live-in duties: shared supervision of years eleven and twelve with two other members of staff, supervision of some morning and evening preps at the main school, weekend duties from time to time.

Each duty in itself was not onerous but, put together, there was little time to prepare lessons, mark books or cover administrative duties. After a month, it was clear that if anything worthwhile was to be achieved, my spirit needed space.

Live-in staff said it was impossible to find accommodation in the area. They'd tried. Even so, with prayer and a belief that something would be available, it was agreed my supervision duties would continue until the end of the current roster.

Focus was required for this position. Personal space was needed in which to move, think and be. And, there was more: an urgent need to be free of live-in duties, to help with commitments back home.

My prayers for a flat were answered. It was in Bowral, a beautiful village of elegant, elderly trees and well-established grand old homes, all with beautiful gardens. My landlords were a caring, elderly couple who'd recently felt prompted to advertise their remaining one-bedroom self-contained flat which they usually kept for family. It was attached to the back of the house. They were a devout, independent, Christian couple, with no church affiliation, who strongly believed in the power of prayer and lived a worshipful life.

They had several self-contained flats in the backyard which they rented, but this one had my name on it. It became a secure, happy home away from home for the rest of my stay. In this blessed space it was possible to revive and concentrate more fully on work and be free to go home of a weekend to meet increasingly heavy family commitments.

My landlords' beautiful garden was their place of worship; their chapel. Inching down its long, cathedral driveway every morning and accelerating into the new day, I'd smile and thank God for the beauty of the day, this life, and pray for wisdom as I drove into a dysfunctional situation, which I was unsure how to resolve and which required diplomacy and patience.

Being a new broom in a school wasn't new, so the accompanying frustrations and often wilful sabotage that came with the territory were no surprise. Staff morale was low and everyone looked over their shoulder. They were overworked, isolated, intimidated and, unfortunately, there was no air in which to complain. The atmosphere was one of recycled fissions vortexing in the claustrophobic staffroom, a symptom of unusual closeness found in boarding schools with their vulnerability to intrusiveness and paranoia.

In contrast to the inspirational drive to school through the breathtakingly beautiful misty mornings, our little classroom was spew-coloured. For me, it mirrored the pervasive sick energy sapping the wonderful potential of this school which was surrounded by sprawling sunlit meadows.

Our classroom had an eastern wall of windows framing a spread of lawn which changed colour throughout the day depending on Mother Nature's moods: ice-blue, clear-coloured mornings morphing into over-ripe, steaming green middays. Fortuitously, when chatting to the handyman, he mentioned there was some leftover powder-blue and white paint in his shed and he could see no reason why we couldn't use it to brighten up the classroom, which we did, in any spare moment, with some help from the handyman.

Another worry was the emotional well-being of the final year boarding students. We had many disagreements. They disclosed how resentful they were of being treated like juniors and they had no meeting place of their own over at the main school.

These independent, outspoken young women needed a common room. These young women back home had responsibilities. Some handled stock, rode motorbikes or horses, checked outlying fences and had boyfriends. Their self-containment and independence of spirit was carved out of childhoods of self-reliance and resilience. Some students appeared more mature than me and some were definitely more experienced.

There was a spare room on the main school campus. While official paranoia opposed its use, the assistance of enthusiastic members of the high school staff, some parents and the students themselves went on to create a warm nest in which to chill while at the main school. Next was to obtain approval for them to have breakfast on the weekends at their boarding quarters. It meant they wouldn't have to be bussed every Saturday and Sunday morning to eat with the juniors. It was agreed that the girls were capable of making their own breakfast.

They could now sit and chat in the sunny, north-eastern, glassed-in back veranda. It gave them much needed autonomy and, for some, it released pent-up emotions.

On one or two occasions when I was off duty, there was the smell of takeaway chicken and the sound of an occasional schoolboy whisper outside the building. The sound of car wheels quietly retreating over gravel was a worry. This was duty 24/7.

While reluctant to leave my precious brood, I needed to resign because of being too thinly stretched. At first my resignation was refused. It was odd having scriptures angrily quoted at me and being told that only the bishop could approve of any such decision. The impression given was that one could not leave. It was not well received when I arranged to see the bishop in Sydney. Perhaps it was meant to present a fearful, insurmountable problem.

The bishop said, 'I'm not God. I can't stop you leaving. If you have to leave, you have to leave and you have my blessing. I hope all goes well for you. God bless you.'

In the meantime, a friend who would soon train to become

a deaconess was keen to apply for the position even after being well briefed. For her, it, too, was only ever going to be a temporary appointment.

Near the end of term, while preparing to return to Sydney, news came of a sudden, unexpected vacancy. It was suggested I apply.

It was sad leaving my delightful students and staff and caring landlords in the beautiful Southern Highlands. The R10 was packed so full it was difficult to see through the rear-vision mirror and equally difficult to see my sister, who'd been staying for a few days and who now sat in the front passenger seat looking like a packhorse.

'The Briars', SCEGGS, Southern Highlands, NSW.

38
A Necessary Education

The next day, I started teaching at a new school because it still had a few days left before end of term. Sadly, a fifth grade vacancy occurred because of a sudden illness and subsequent death of a beloved member of staff. I was to be her replacement at Ingleholme, Turramurra, an annexe of PLC, Pymble.

When I arrived, it was important to walk respectfully and slipper-quiet around their mountain of grief. Under those conditions, it was difficult for them to be effusive in their welcome.

I missed the staff and students at Moss Vale but was thankful to be home with family. Stan's emphysema had worsened. Ruby was relieved to have another pair of hands and a spare driver. There was no downtime.

The mistress in charge, Miss P, who was so totally devoted to her staff and students, and so hands-on, often summoned me into her office, door closed, followed by a reprimand for a misdemeanour or two, such as daring to move a bookcase in my classroom without her permission. Most principals would be annoyed if you involved them in such trivialities. But it was a measure of the woman when, in time, she trusted me to rearrange whatever.

Smokers weren't allowed in this particular staffroom in the days before smoking was prohibited. The younger members of staff were inclined to sit outside the staff room on kindergarten chairs, squashed into a small corner under an awning where I, quite unexpectedly, gained a rich sex education amid drifts of smoke and much laughter.

Smoke signals announced the latest news and it wasn't always good. One colleague had just discovered that her husband was a closet homosexual. The handsome hunk he'd brought back with him from his holiday in Italy, and who'd been staying with them for the past few months, was, in fact, his lover.

'What's a homosexual?' I asked.

'You can't be serious?'

I was. It was only natural then that the conversation turned to talk about lesbians.

'What's a lesbian?'

On another day there was talk of tampons, a new hygienic offering. Some said they found them to be an improvement.

I said, 'But I can't see how they work.'

'You put them inside.'

'Where?'

'Oh, dear,' said one colleague. 'Come home. I'll stand outside the loo and shout instructions.'

We roared at the idea and one or two nearly fell off their kindergarten chairs.

My helpful colleague stood on one side of the closed door to the loo and shouted instructions. Location, location, location. I, on the other side of the door, struggled to locate. I won't go into the instructions, some of which I hardly heard myself, because we were laughing so much.

After many failed attempts, my disbelieving colleague expressed concern that, as I was soon to be married, I needed to familiarise myself with my anatomy. She suggested I buy a large magnifying mirror and set out on a solitary, exploratory mission to the South Pole.

*

Shower Tea

There is collusion from the moment
she enters the sisters' covenant,
from those who rush
happy-ever-after, dear.
They shower her with gift-wrapped roles,
flowers-wed-bred,
which Time unravels.
Some bouquets have thorns.

39
A Troublesome Attitude

The wedding date was only weeks away. G and I discussed our need to look for a place to rent. A friend from church rang me to say she and her sister were looking for someone to take over the lease of their large, sunny, two-bedroomed flat on the main road in Penshurst Street, Willoughby North.

I knew the flat well. It faced east and was full of light. Whenever visiting, I always imagined a large vase of flowers on a small table underneath the corner window, never thinking that one day it would be just like that. 'We're so lucky.' I wanted to shout out our good fortune. We couldn't have asked for a better location: shops, transport, close to family, friends and church. We could save because the rent was reasonable. We discussed banking my salary so we could buy land and build as soon as possible. But it seemed I was the only one celebrating.

We pulled up outside G's place.

'Don't say anything to Mum. I'll have to pick the right time… make it up to her, somehow.'

'What do you mean? We didn't say we were going to live with her, did we?'

Judging by the silence in the car, someone had.

'I'll handle it.'

'It's just after what Mum and Dad have been through, I'd really like to start out on our own. Perhaps later –'

I told my parents about how guilty I felt. 'Am I being selfish?'

Ruby said,' You're doing the right thing.'

Stan said, 'Too right.'

Apparently, it was presumed that we would live with J, who'd been widowed for nearly two years. Even if we had decided to live with her, it was a two-bedroom brick bungalow and we would have the small, single, second bedroom. The main problem for me was the situation would be an all too familiar double-edged sword. I knew what it was like. And I was really looking forward to having some space of our own.

My great grandmother had always lived with Stan and Ruby. This set a precedent for the widowed, lonely and needy. Bachelor prisoners of war, maiden aunts, widowed aunts and uncles, neglected children and more, slept on our back veranda or we shared bedrooms. One family in need pitched a tent in our backyard for over a year while they waited for public housing. I was used to sharing bedrooms, bathrooms, toilets, kitchens and territories.

We shared more than food around the table. There were half-baked opinions, battered beliefs, tall tasty tales and peels of laughter from those who stayed on for seconds. Any leftovers, such as pain or fear or tears, were swiftly swept under the table while disputes were whisked well away from the impressionable young.

My fiancé and I discussed plans for the honeymoon. He wanted to know what I would like to do; a promising start. I explained that because I was overtired and had lost weight during the year, I needed to chill. It'd been a frantic year: changes of school, whirlpool of reports, preparation for end of year open day activities, concerts, shower teas, sewing my bridal dress and my sister's bridesmaid's dress, Christmas festivities and helping Ruby look after two grandchildren full-time.

'First of all, can we have a few really quiet days? It's been hectic.' I imagined swimming, strolling along the beach, hand in hand, falling into champagne sands, watching a salmon sun draw curtains at the close of a summer's day. 'What about you?'

'I'd like to do a bit of travelling.'

Agreed. Rest and then some travelling.

The groom wanted the honeymoon to be a surprise. It soon became a state secret. When I heard that the best man had been co-opted to assist with the itinerary, I felt uncomfortable but supposed it was because I'd expected we'd plan our honeymoon together. The groom was an highly efficient schedules clerk with Urban Transit Authority. He spent his days organising time and labour to the nth degree. On a quiet day, his friend was nothing less than a fully stoked steam engine, a draughtsman, who worked in fine detail. My uncomfortable feeling wouldn't go away. How could the plans be checked without offending the very excited him and without seeming to be a spoilsport?

My fiancé hugged me. 'Sweetheart, it's been planned very carefully.'

'That's what worries me. Why so much planning? How come D's involved?'

As a left-hander, I didn't know what my right-hander was doing and it was a difficult adjustment. My instinct was not happy with arrangements but there was no direct evidence to justify my unsettled feeling, until – Big Ears overheard a snippet about the honeymoon the week before the wedding.

Ruby was asking her future son-in-law, in hushed tones, 'It's the social pages. They like to give the readers an inkling –'

'Touring. The Barossa Valley.'

Were there beaches in the Barossa Valley? And why so far? Travelling west in January, in my non-air-conditioned car?

I walked into the kitchen. 'Touring? Barossa Valley? I hope not.'

Ruby said, 'Now don't go spoiling –'

The groom grinned.

'The beach?'

'Of course, sweetheart. Pack swimmers.'

It's the day before the wedding. Still have to buy a going-away outfit. I delayed buying it because I believed I didn't need one.

We're staying overnight in the honeymoon suite at the reception centre. No need to change. But tradition was glaring at me, wearing me down. The family eccentric was such a disappointment when questioning anything traditional. It was as if the reception roof was being tempted to cave in should this important going-away outfit be skipped. Then I had to organise something old, something new, something borrowed, something blue.

'Who says I have to do all this?'

'Now don't start,' says Ruby as I turn the car, probably too quickly, into a parking spot. And mother of the bride is out of the car headed towards Grace Bros. She is lights, energy, action.

I drag up the rear. My legs are full of lead. We walk into the post-Christmas crush. Sale. Sale. Sale. Up the escalators. Mezzanine floor. Stockings. Make-up. Buying a going-away outfit is going to be a problem. I've lost so much weight in the past year that I really don't know what to wear.

We don't find anything suitable in Grace Bros so cross the road and head for our favourite boutique in Victoria Avenue.

Ruby, the ever thoughtful pragmatist, says, 'There must be something in here, although I have to admit there doesn't seem to be much,' the truth being there was even less than not much.

I determine to buy the next outfit, regardless of what it is. The salesgirl shows me the latest in pants suits. Latest fashion. Creamy *guippure* lace.

'Very stylish,' the shop assistant says. 'Just flown in.'

I'd believe it. Could almost hear its wings flapping. Little did I know it was so fashionable that one of the wedding guests would wear an identical outfit. Had I known, we could've started a migration south.

The short lacy sleeves highlight my thin hairy arms and bony elbows. The simple collarless V-neck top accentuates my long thin neck and obvious lack of cleavage. When I turn side on and look in the mirror, my shoulder blades are more prominent than my breasts. This ugly, expensive outfit will be given away to a worthy cause at the earliest possible convenience.

Ruby says, 'Looks very, very nice. Do you like it?'

'It'll do.'

'Only if you like it.'

'Mum, you know what I think about –'

'I don't want to hear.' Ruby almost strangles her handbag.

The shop assistant walks away.

I whisper. 'This whole marriage thing is obscene. Why wear a veil?' I'd recently learnt about another symbolic interpretation of the bridal veil. I whisper, 'Why draw attention to a woman's hymen in public?' I love using biological terms.

Ruby shakes her head. 'The things you say. There's no need to be so crude.'

'Mum, somebody's got to say it. If you ask me, what's crude is having to wear a veil in the first place. I can't believe we do it.' But I know I'm doing it to please my parents, rellies and friends.

Ruby swivels her chair and faces the door. Her handbag gasps for air. 'I don't want to hear…good enough for your mother –'

'I know, I know. I'm just saying. All that symbolism for the woman on her wedding day. It's disgusting.'

'Symbol-what? On second thoughts, I don't want to know.' Ruby stands up taller than her five feet.

The ponytailed shop assistant tosses her head and glares at me when she hands me the generously wrapped box of glad rags. She smiles at Ruby. 'Oh, everyone loves a wedding, don't they? I hope you have an absolutely fabulous time. It's such an exciting time, isn't it?'

We all smile.

'Thank you,' I say, aware that politeness has a currency of its own and this exchange is costing me squillions.

I'd been aware of my troublesome attitude for sometime now. No one was forcing me to marry. It was my decision but where joint decisions were to be made about our plans in the future it seemed to be that I had to follow plans made on my behalf by my better half. Why did you have to hand over your person?

About six weeks before the wedding, I notice an indescribable feeling late one afternoon while kneeling on the bedroom floor, cutting out my wedding dress. It's unusually quiet; a rare instance in our house. As I cut into metres of delustred satin I become aware of an emotion hovering somewhere between me and the white satin: a transparent darkness. I try looking into it to see it for what it is. What's the problem?

It feels as though part of me has walked away. Is it a grieving process? Something about losing my independence? The emotion gives the feeling that someone dear is no longer there. Is it God turning away? My spirit? The silence in the house gives it a voice. What's there to understand about this? I pin patterns, conscious of a puzzling, emotional, hovering void.

That night, I dream. It soon turns into a nightmare. I'm sitting in the passenger's seat of my car when someone leans onto the bonnet and aims at me. Looks like a gun. Are they going to shoot me? I realise I'm dreaming. I rewind the horror. I wake shaking.

Another night. Another nightmare. My fiancé is driving and we drive straight into blackness. It looks like we're heading into the back of a truck. Will we crash? I realise it's a dream and quickly rewind the ending, just before running into the black void of a truck.

I kept a particular fear of the void and the occasional nightmare to myself until one afternoon I had to speak the unspeakable. 'Mum, I've got this awful feeling. It's horrible. I can't describe it. It's as though, as though –' There were no words. Feeling was below expression. 'I know this is a huge thing to say but I feel there's something not right. I'm worried but I don't know –' Up until now I had avoided telling Ruby because I was worried about how she'd react.

But she was calm personified. She smiled. 'I've been waiting for this. You've got wedding jitters, that's all. Everybody gets them.'

'Really?' I desperately needed to believe her. The invitation scrolls had been posted only a few days earlier and the wedding was six weeks away. 'It's just this feeling. Won't go away. I really don't think I should –'

Ruby put her teacup down in such a way that had I been able

to describe the feeling her cup might well have broken the saucer. 'You think too much. That's your problem. Goodness me, I couldn't believe I was going to marry your father. I couldn't believe I'd be sitting opposite him at the breakfast table.'

'Well, do you know what I see? A mediaeval institution. A romantic, paternalistic couple front. Good for the economy.'

'I should've guessed. On your high horse again.' Ruby started to leave the room, hand in hand with disgust.

'We follow a script,' I called after her. 'We're programmed but the program is flawed. Can't you see? Hey, everyone, roll up, roll up, quick, sign here while there's still lust in your loins.'

On the surface, things seemed to flow smoothly between GB and me but I was aware of a subterranean current. It was pulling me, trying to tell me something. But I reasoned it was as Ruby had suggested. Probably just having difficulty accommodating another's way; not used to following. I could see what she was saying but I was used to compromising and negotiating in other aspects of my life. In fact, it was seen to be one of my strengths.

Before we married, we were obliged to attend marriage counselling classes run by the Anglican church. Chastity was discussed. It was important to remain chaste. We had no problem there. I admired my fiancé's restraint on matters sexual until he said one night before the wedding, 'Passion can make you do things you don't want. We don't really need it.' Was he channelling Ruby? She couldn't have said it any better. She would've added the scary bit, though, which I knew off by heart: 'It can creep up behind you and grab you. You don't want that.'

Wedding vows were discussed. On principle, I couldn't agree with the vow 'to obey'. What if the decision made by the husband was clearly not in the best interests of his wife or family? What then? What if –? To submit, to yield because of an archaic vow, seemed unintelligible.

We discussed when to start a family. I had no doubt about my maternal drive. It was high tide: an historical, biological high tide. I was ready to start and be totally committed to raising a loving family, expecting to replicate Stan and Ruby's example – marriage based on love, trust and mutual respect; always looking in the same direction.

It was a pragmatic decision to make my wedding gown. I didn't have much time but the overpriced ready-made ones made the decision for me. In the busy school weeks leading up to the wedding, I struggled to keep afloat, deep in a sea of fabric. I was never a happy sewer. I didn't like being around myself when I sewed, drafted patterns, rescued hyperventilating fabrics and swore. This was normal behaviour when sewing or whenever I knocked over the pin tin again or lost the good scissors. I growled whenever I refilled bobbins. I didn't sew much these days. Studying and teaching had been all-consuming.

When in use, the sewing machine was usually set up at one end of the kitchen table or on a card table in the sunroom. But, these days, every room in house was full. Ruby was looking after two grandchildren from breakfast until dinner, supposedly part-time. A widowed uncle slept in the sunroom. There was really only one place left to sew and that was in the bedroom I shared with my sister. The machine was set up at the end of the bed on the suggestion of a desk, which had been my first lay-by: a small Nock and Kirby student's desk. I bought it at the same time I bought a small typewriter when I worked in the city.

An old white sheet was spread out on motley green carpet so as to protect the fabric from any dust. I still am a fussy sewer, always washing hands so as not to leave grease on fabric or pattern. I like my scissors sharp. Once I start sewing, should any person be foolish enough to come near me they risk having their edges clipped by my pinking-sheared attitude.

The latch on the bedroom door was loose with age. A falling feather could open it. It was summer school holidays and often two little helpers, my niece and nephew, Kim and Matthew, would wander into the bedroom. 'Watcha doin', Aunny Anne?' They'd kneel on the floor beside me and lean their little sweaty hands on swaths of delustred satin and guipure lace.

One humid afternoon, after we spilt the pin tin a second time and after we picked up each pin and put them back into the tin, we stood up, held clammy hands and decided go visit Nanny in the kitchen.

'Hello, Nanny,' I clipped. 'Watcha doin'?'

Nanny was busy. She was draining boiled potatoes. We stood nearby, listened to the water roar down the plug hole, runaway to the ocean. We watched steam rise from the hot potatoes and escape through the large open window.

'Mum, every day this week…too much.'

'Patience…something you don't have –'

'Can't you say we're too busy?'

Ruby turned down the gas. She checked the sausages under the griller and rolled them over, at the same time suggesting I do something useful. Bath the children or mash the potatoes. The children were having an early tea. Their grandmother wanted them fed and ready for bed when their parents arrived. 'They'll be tired after a long day.'

I mashed the potatoes. 'Can't you say?'

'No. I will not. You're the one with – it's not my fault if – if they – if you –'

'I know, I know, but I'm screaming inside. Look.' I shut my eyes tight, opened my mouth wide, Easter-clown-show-like and swivelled my head from side to side. Mouthed H-E-L-P.

It looked funny. The children thought so, too. They laughed. Nanny didn't. Her lips had disappeared. Perhaps she was screaming too.

40
For Better or for Worse

> God be in my head and in my understanding
> God be in mine eyes and in my looking
> God be in my mouth and in my speaking
> God be in mine heart and in my thinking
> God be at mine end and in my departing.
>
> Old English prayer

We married on 8 January 1971, at St Stephen's Anglican Church, Willoughby. The processional was Purcell's Trumpet Voluntary, which foretold the coming celebration and the sacredness of our wedding vows. My sister sang of endless love, Bach's 'Jesu Joy of Man's desiring…' The choir sang a prayer for us, 'God be in my head…' set by John Rutter. The recessional, Vidor's Toccata, trumpeted the promises made of love and commitment. The carillon rang our intentions into the community on a crystal-clear summer's night. My sixth-grade students formed a surprise guard of honour, squealing with delight as they threw rose petals and coloured rice at the bride and groom. There was no doubt our union was showered with many blessings.

The reception was held close by, within walking distance, at Windsor Gardens, a grand Victorian mansion which welcomed many grooms and brides. The reception followed convention. The lady-in-waiting directed us. We were always in the right place at the right time, and smiled, smiled, smiled. At the end of 'Wish me luck as you wave me goodbye', she hovered and then handed the groom the keys to the honeymoon suite. 'The night's young,' she said and winked at him.

As we drove out the circular driveway, pretending we were driving somewhere else, guests cheered and waved and cans rattled. As husband and wife, we laughed and chatted, both very pleased it had gone so well. 'Wasn't it's funny when… What about uncle…'

Fifteen or so minutes later, we were a few miles away, at Forestville, near the old 'blinking light'. It was close to where the best man and his wife lived in a red- brick, blue-tiled, triple-fronted home. The groom stopped the car. We were only a few miles away from the glittering hem of the Pacific Ocean. I could almost feel its cool shifting sands beneath my feet.

The groom tapped the steering wheel as we sat in the car parked by the side of the road. If we went down the hill and turned left, we'd head towards Narrabeen and Newport. If we went straight ahead, we could end up at Dee Why, Collaroy or Long Reef. To our right, not too far away, was Balmoral, a friendly grin of a beach.

'I don't mind which way we go,' I said. 'Which way do you think?'

It really didn't matter which beach. What mattered was just being together, walking hand in hand, in the same direction, on a starry night. That'd be both romantic and a good start: a positive pattern to lay down for the bigger things that were to come, things we'd have to face as a couple. Like Stan and Ruby, I, too, wanted to share the simple pleasures in life that would make us rich. Life was in the pattern which was there in everyday detail; the tiniest thing created the patterns in life. Here we were, man and wife, giving birth to a brand-new one, the subtext of life. Now, as a couple, I was conscious of us drafting our own pattern.

'It's going to be hard,' Ruby had said. 'You'll both have to adjust. At times, it's more give than take.'

Sitting in the passenger seat of my car, unsure of why we'd stopped, puzzled by a non-committal response from the groom, there was an ever so slight feeling of confusion. Was it just me? Or did he feel it too?'

'We'd better get back,' he said. 'Everyone should be gone by now.'

'Oh, a walk along the beach'd be nice.'

'We'd better get back.'

I'd imagined a sort of kicking up of heels; young lovers looking up at the Milky Way, looking for the Saucepan, the Southern Cross; just being there, marvelling at us just being there, being with the ebb and flow of tide.

'Could we just pop down to the water?'

'What, with all those perverts?'

'Perverts? Where? I've never seen any.'

The groom turned on the ignition and carried out an unexpected U-turn. 'I've got an idea.'

'What is it?'

'You'll see.'

I was the only one aware that my spirit was actually heading downhill, towards the coast, so, in a sense, there was one less person in the car. I had to drag myself back and remind myself that as a bride, whose identity from this time forward would be through him, for I had taken his name, I needed to relax and put on my patience hat. It always seemed odd when it said that marriage was when two people became one. But if two equalled one, then surely someone in the couple, or parts of both in the couple, became less than. I expected marriage to be like Stan and Ruby's, where one plus one equalled two and they were worth more than their sum.

We cruised along Victoria Avenue, Chatswood, until we pulled up outside a milk bar. He visibly relaxed. This was where he wanted to be. We walked in and my husband asked if I'd like an orange juice. He kept looking around as if expecting to see someone. We sat down.

'They wouldn't believe it if they saw us now.' He laughed.

I'd have laughed, too, if I'd thought it was funny. I agreed. No one would guess. Just a few blocks away, at 39 Artarmon Road, they'd be celebrating and it was highly unlikely anyone would be sitting at a small table sipping orange juice out of waxy, striped straws.

The first day of the honeymoon we travelled south, away from the coast. My husband knew where we were going. I plastered an artificial smile on my face. This man beside me, driving my car, was to be my partner for the rest of my life, yet I still didn't know where I was going.

I told myself to be patient and not spoil the big surprise. It's just that I would really liked to have known where we were headed. Wasn't half the fun in the planning, in the dreaming? What with the Barossa Valley and neither of us wine buffs, I was curious. I'd just have to be patient.

Around mid-morning, we pulled up outside one of the groomsmen's homes in Moss Vale. He was a rail enthusiast and a close friend. His wife had been very kind to me when I worked in Moss Vale. She was unable to come to the wedding because their first born was due any day. They were expecting us and we sat down to delicious, celebratory morning tea. Lunch was in Canberra, at another of the groom's friends, another rail enthusiast, whose wife was very ill. They, too, were expecting us and we sat down to a scrumptious salad and dessert.

By mid-afternoon we were heading south, driving further away from the coast. Apparently we were running late so drove past the setting sun and into the night. We arrived on the southern side of Cooma around ten o'clock. I didn't know Cooma had beaches but I thought to myself patience, patience. I was so tired. It felt more like a dream state than reality.

Tucked up in bed, the driver studied the itinerary.

'Can I have a look?' I reached out.

There was a huff and a puff. Somehow my request offended him. What had I said? Apologising for I didn't know what, I explained how I'd like to know where we were going each day. I studied the itinerary. Fourteen nights of pre-booked motels.

'D said you get two nights free that way.'

'It looks like we're on the move every day.'

'We'll need an early start in the morning.'

'But it's not what we – I don't know – this means we're travelling everyday. I mean –'

'There are two nights at Philip Island.' The tone of voice was one of concession.

'How far away is that?' I checked the itinerary and didn't sleep well that night. The yoke of disappointment was heavy. It seemed someone was heading in the right direction but it wasn't me. I just wanted to stop. Needed to stop. Now. Not in a week's time.

Constant travel and I were never the best of friends. Travelling west in summer, in a non-air-conditioned car, was not my idea of a honeymoon. I soon discovered there were marvellous opportunities for photo stops by railway lines, railway stations, stationmaster's cottages and goods sheds. Railway lines snaked their way around the hills; perfect photo opportunities. Sometimes, as we sat and waited in the midday sun, the train ran late. At other times we searched for abandoned railway lines. Meantime, the fulsome arms of the January sun wrapped themselves around us.

It's midday. We reach Hill End, find the Gold Rush Museum and look at the memorabilia. My head's pounding. I find shade in the lavatory; in the please-can-you-at-least-clean-me-once-a-week-and-leave-me-some-toilet-paper-next-time-loo. It feels like I might have a chill in the bladder. There's not much relief in here but it's cooler. The flies think so too.

Over the next few days, whenever we stopped I headed straight for the ladies' loo and would sit there trying to escape the heat as well as cope with a stinging, uncomfortable urge to pee. My body mirrored the ache in the landscape. Heat shimmered off the backs of sun-struck cattle and forlorn sheep roasted in shadeless, dehydrated paddocks.

As we entered the Barossa Valley, I resented the fact that we were only ever going to be on one track. GB feigned surprise, surprise, whenever we happened, fortuitously, to stumble upon another abandoned line. While in the Barossa Valley, we sought out every possible branch line and there were several. These branched off from a main passenger line which had ceased service. I could understand why.

GB's exclamations regarding serendipity had become a predictable pattern. 'Oh, look, sweetheart, we might just be in time to catch the ABC123KYD697 on the up-down-over-under-and-around line or we might see the XYZ500PTO348 on the up-down-upside-down-over-and-around line.'

By now I was feeling uncomfortable in the presence of my companion's mood swings. They seemed to depend on daily events. If there was a glitch or delay, it would be taken personally. More often than not, Thomas the Tank Engine and his friends ran late. I wished I was brave enough to hop into the driver's seat, turn the car around and head east, where we'd find ever faithful sunrises kissing the Pacific. We could start again. But the atmosphere had a fragility. I learnt to pre-test my every word and gesture.

There was no doubt the schedules clerk and the draughtsman excelled themselves in their planning. The trip must have required considerable know-how. There was the coordination of different states' rail gauges and they had to keep in mind all the variables, such as different time zones. Grand photographic opportunities proved to be well considered.

The groom was an excellent photographer. He used a heavy German camera which required fine focusing. It was a delicate piece of equipment and the adjustments took time. During this delicate procedure, I'm sure the sun moved and shadows lengthened. Two cameras took the same photo, one after the other. It took me days to realise the second camera belonged to D. So, in a sense, he did come with us.

My increasing resentment could have ripped up the nearest railway line with one hand, no matter how significant or how historical or how abandoned, but my increasing weariness prevented me from doing so. I learnt it was important to keep an even temperature inside the car by showing enthusiasm in all activities.

We stopped at a lookout, Annie's Lookout. I posed, hand to head: Annie, looking out to the far horizon. That's when I saw the coastline. I inhaled. Was that sweet fragrance a coastal breeze?

We travelled on the Great Ocean Road. Took photographs of the Twelve Apostles. They towered above inaccessible sandy beaches, found at the foot of tall cliffs. At Philip Island we stayed two nights. Sand under my feet. The fairy penguins came in after dusk, wave after wave of them, arriving full-bellied, exhausted. We sat on observers' seats in spotting rain. We watched the wondrous creatures waddle up the beach to their damp burrows where they fed their young.

One day, before we left from heaven-knows-where, we drove around a small southern town where I glimpsed the hint of a fishing bay. The driver looked for a rise which would indicate an old embankment but without success. As we drove back and forth, a personal storm brewed inside the car. Lightning flashed. The frustrated one slapped the steering wheel, again and again. My inner self was fleeing and my imaginary steering wheel and I trembled at the outbursts.

Surprisingly, I found the elusive, abandoned embankment on the same site as the abandoned tennis court. Success was due to the desperate act of a desperate woman. As we drove away from the fishing village, I was having to quieten my racing heart and face reality. This so-called honeymoon was one filled with increasing unease. I felt as if I'd been filleted and bled back into the bay.

On the last leg home, we walked onto a beach near Boyd Town, a little village, a whaling port. My companion wasn't interested in walking along the ocean's edge so I suggested he go and explore the historical site without me. I'd be fine. I was feeling uncomfortable and wasn't eating properly. My mouth was constantly dry. I was light-headed and suspected I had a fever. There were other problems, too, so I walked along the main street until I found a chemist.

After I told her my situation, she asked if I was on my honeymoon. I was surprised. Was it the shine on my new wedding ring? She told me about the honeymooner's UTI and gave me measures for relief. Walking out of the pharmacy, I wondered why no one had ever mentioned it.

I sit opposite my husband in a restaurant in a south coast motel. I listen to him recall the day's events. It's as if he's talking to someone else. I suspect it's D and I'm the dry run. It frightens me to feel so far away, yet we sit so close. He relives the day while I wait for it to start.

Waves of panic. I look out the window and strain my eyes, desperate to connect with something, anything. I need to connect now, connect quickly. Hibiscus. Yes. Cadmium-blue highlights. I gaze at the sparkles on the pool; mirrored starlight. A family splashes. Playful laughter. I gaze at the ripples on the surface until I become its lap-lap, lap-lap.

I face fear and turn to observe the groom who's emptying his plate. At this point, my soon-to-be constant companion, loneliness, walks in, recognises me, comes over, sits beside me and holds me tight.

Mr and Mrs G.J. Bedwin, 1971.

41

Snail Mail

We were renting a flat in Penshurst Street when we were offered subsidised rent to live in a home at Forestville and look after it while the owners were overseas. One of the owners was a theologian and author. He was taking up a lecturing post for twelve months. He offered us the use of his library: a powerhouse in the third bedroom of this small, three-bedroom weatherboard home in a quiet cul-de-sac. Ahead of me was a feast of philosophy, soul food and biography; my dream library.

Just a few months into our caretaking/renting mode, in this inspirational home filled with fine antique oil paintings and refined French-polished furniture and indoor plants that ran freely, flourishing along window tops, I nearly burnt the house down.

There'd been an early morning chill. When we were eating breakfast, warmed by a small two-bar radiator, the power failed. It was a general blackout. Before we left for work, I put the radiator back in its rightful place in the gap between the stove and kitchen cabinet.

About an hour or two later, I was standing in the classroom teaching percentages to sixth grade when a sweeping sickness overtook me. I knew I couldn't stay. Had to go. No choice. Straight away. Hurry. Hurry. No idea why I was sick. Fifteen minutes ago, I felt fine. Raced home, desperate to get there.

When I walked in the front door, lights were on and there was the smell of burning wood. I ran to the kitchen. The radiator was aglow, both bars blazing, and the wooden side of the kitchen cabinet was also aglow. Heart pounding, I turned off the heater and pulled it out, fearful of the next stage – flames. But I was just in time. I watched the wood on the side cupboard fade from blazing red and turn into a wall of matt black ash. It held its place until I touched it. Thankfully there were no flames. 'Thank you, Lord, thank you.'

I put the radiator in the laundry on top of the cupboard and pushed it out of sight. It wasn't mine to throw out. The real estate agent was respectful when I reported it, even though I felt like an irresponsible fool. I shivered till it hurt. I rang the boss and told her what had happened, said I was well again and asked if it was too late to come back to school.

'My dear girl, you've had an awful fright. I don't want you driving in that condition.'

The overwhelming sickness had gone and was no longer a mystery. This sacred home had comprehensive prayer insurance.

It was during our year at Forestville that I had my first false alarm. Considering the ease with which Ruby had fallen pregnant, I assumed, being her daughter, that it would be easy for me too. But months had passed without success.

I was teaching full-time and had become so weak and nauseated I thought I might be pregnant. I was always regular, could set the clock, almost to the hour. Now overdue, I felt no excitement. Too sick for that. As I was new in the area, I had to see a new doctor. We chatted for a few minutes. No physical examination and few questions asked. The pregnancy test proved negative, as suspected.

'If I'm not pregnant, I wonder why I feel so sick and have all this pain. I'm losing weight and can't afford to lose any more.'

The doctor informed me that many young women suffered anxiety early in their marriage because they weren't used to responsibility.

I smiled, always a good delaying tactic when trying to buy more time to contain flashes of indignation. 'I'm quite used to responsibility.'

It was the doctor's turn to smile. He seemed amused. He proceeded to write out a script for Valium and gave me a medical certificate for three weeks' sick leave because of what he believed was an anxiety state.

'I think there's something wrong with me physically.'

'Yes, yes,' he nodded and showed me out.

Monthly pain certainly had a history and it was getting worse. Over the years, I'd wake in the middle of the night in pain and the attacks were more frequent. My former GP explained that because I was unmarried there could be no internal examination. No ultrasounds in those days.

I liked my GP. His wife worked in the same practice. She was always fully booked. Doctor S spoke positively about women in the workplace. But the day I arrived with an engagement ring on my finger, he was not impressed. I told him I was getting married in two months' time and needed a script for the contraceptive pill. He pushed his chair back, folded his arms, frowned into his lap. Silence. Surely he wasn't going to refuse.

Theoretically, the pill was only supposed to be given to married women but I was getting married in a few months' time and friends said it was best to deal with the nausea before the wedding. The plan was I'd take the pill for six months and then we'd start a family.

Dr S lifted his head. 'I want you to listen to this very carefully. Anyone can get married but not everyone can have a career. For some women, marriage is a wasteland. You've got a career ahead of you.'

I was speechless. What did he know about my work? It wasn't until years later I learnt he was on the school board where I taught. He might have assumed I knew but I didn't. But he'd unwittingly touched a raw spot. I'd been conflicted about marriage since I was old enough to understand its patriarchal origins. I was appalled to learn that, historically, women were listed as property along with the cows and men were their guardians.

A colleague had recently spoken to me like Dr S. It was Mrs H, an older, much trusted, gifted colleague. 'Buy yourself a nice unit...you've got a career ahead.' Ruby never liked the sound of Mrs H because she was a divorcee and because she was always encouraging her daughter to do shameless things, like buy a unit.

No one in our family had a career. You had a job. Women were expected to give up their jobs once they married in order to fulfil their destiny: wife, mother, housekeeper, social secretary.

I took Dr S's prescription with mixed feelings.

'Give it more thought,' he said. 'Never too late.' He walked me to the door and held it open and mumbled, 'I hope you'll be happy.'

I expected to be. When Ruby heard what he'd said, she said, 'How dare he!'

In a way, I agreed with her. I had to admit it did come as bit of a shock.

Three weeks off work made no difference. In fact, I felt worse. I rang the practice again and asked to see another doctor. Fortunately, this doctor was both a GP and gynaecologist. On internal examination, he diagnosed either an advanced fallopian tube pregnancy or a large ovarian cyst. Either way, I needed urgent surgery. Within two days, I was in Chatswood Community Hospital and had a large ovarian cyst removed. It was chocolate-coloured and its history showed that it was twelve years old and had haemorrhaged twice.

The head sister said, 'I've never seen anyone go into surgery looking so grey and come out looking so rosy.'

A week later, I was allowed out of hospital on the proviso that I convalesce in someone's care. So my husband and I stayed with my parents for a week. Ruby was caring and watchful. She kept bringing me in cups of tea and biscuits and tempting nibblies. I had substantial weight to gain now that the toxins had gone.

Because the double bed divan on which we slept was folded away every morning and turned back into a lounge during the day, I often rested on my parents' bed.

Ruby came in one day and rummaged in her wardrobe.

'What are you looking for?'

'I have something to give you. I think it's safe – it really belongs to you. I didn't know when to – I feel guilty but –'

She handed me a large brown envelope. It was official-looking. 'On Her Majesty's Service, Teachers College, Armidale.' I recognised the handwriting.

'I didn't give it to you at the time because I thought it might unsettle –'

'How long have you had it?'

'Ohhh, when you were in Moss Vale, it –'

Almost two years. Snail mail, indeed. I opened the envelope and pulled out a stapled A4, duplicate or triplicate of a manuscript. On its cover it read, 'Banyan'. I opened it and on the first page he'd written, 'Dear Anne, / that you may / better understand how I think and / why I act as I do. / Edwin / P.'

Ruby said, 'I've been waiting for the right time.'

'What do you mean? Why didn't you give it to me earlier?'

'Because it might've unsettled –'

'Isn't that for me to –?'

'I don't want it causing any trouble. You won't act on it, will you?'

'Mu-um. The deed's done, isn't it? It's a bit late to reply.'

'Just so long as you remember, there's no turning back. You're a married woman.'

'Was I when this arrived?'

'You needn't go on about it.'

I waited for Ruby to leave the room before reading the introduction and the poems with themes of life: love, death, beauty, nature.

My unsettled mother found reasons to come into the bedroom. 'Haven't you put that thing away yet? You'd better put it away before your husband gets home. What are you going to do with it? You've got no use for it.'

Ruby was right about one thing. My husband would've been very upset had he found me reading the manuscript. Unbeknownst to me, at this stage, he was reading my private pre- and post-marriage journals.

We were both surprised when, some months later, I found him sitting on his side of our bed engrossed in something.

'What are you reading?'

He was reading one of my journals. I startled him when I spoke. 'Why are you reading –? If you want to read one, then please ask… I've got nothing to hide.'

He stood up as if over me. 'Why do you do it? I suppose you're writing about me.'

I'd never thought about journal writing affecting someone else. I could understand, now, why Beatrix Potter journalled in code.

'How would you feel if I decided to go through your private things, like your briefcase or wallet, without asking? It's a bit like that.'

'But you're doing this secretly.'

'It's not a secret. It's private. There's a difference. It's just something I do.'

I couldn't understand his escalation in mood. What could be done to soothe the glaring whites of his eyes? In a slow, low-key voice, 'Put it this way. It's a courtesy, a common courtesy to ask.'

So, for peace's sake, and Paranoid's, I stopped journalling. Was this another unspoken boundary instituted within marriage or was it only in mine? When the schedules clerk went to work, I gathered all the journals and put them in the incinerator and burnt them. There was no use throwing them into the bin. The man of the house liked to rummage through the garbage bin mostly on a daily basis.

Some years later, my husband and I came to Sydney for the weekend. It was Saturday morning and his usual practice was to head into town for a few hours. I sat at the kitchen table beside my father and flicked through the *North Shore Times* while he did the morning crossword. I liked to keep in touch with home events and people. There was one page with a big hole in it.

'Dad, what's this bit?'

'Blowed if I know. Your mother'll know.'

It must've been something important for Ruby to cut out. I went inside and asked. There was reticence and she was clearly annoyed.

Later, Ruby appeared with the missing piece and handed it over. It was a piece about the poet and a poetry anthology, *Banyan*.

'I thought – knowing – I thought it better –'

'Mu-um.'

Edwin J Wilson lived and worked in Sydney; married with

children. This was his first poetry publication. After I read it, Ruby took the piece of paper back and worried it between her fingers before folding it into four and burying it deep in her apron pocket.

Considering the degree of her concern, I shouldn't have teased, but part of me was serious. 'Wouldn't mind buying a copy. I could compare it with his earlier manuscript. That'd be interesting.'

'Don't tell me you've still got that thing. You should've got rid of it by now.'

I leant back in my chair and smiled. 'Well, fancy that. Still writing. Good on him. What do you reckon, Dad?'

'Nothing to do with me, Twerpo.'

Banyan by E.J. Wilson.

42

For Two Years –

I was the epitome of 'wives, obey your husbands'. I left Sydney holding hands with my very own head of the house.

We looked at buying a triple-fronted, white weatherboard with dark blue downpipes, matching gutters and tastefully coordinated eaves. We stood there, on our second viewing, on the plush, soft as velvet, freshly mown bent with blue couch lawn. We discussed whether to buy No. 7 or not. This would be our first home. We'd sold our land in aspirational Belrose. For the same price we could buy house and land in Newcastle. As the agent performed his sales routine, I found myself humming, 'Little boxes, little boxes… There's a blue one and a green one…'

For some time, I'd been fighting an inner resistance to sell our block of land but I reasoned it could be for the best. At least, moving north for two years would give us a chance to deepen our relationship, which seriously lacked intimate communication and teamwork.

The real estate agent said this house was in one of the best streets of Newcastle. 'Transfers like to buy in this area because it's easy resale if you have to transfer again, in a year or two.'

We nodded. Good point that.

Earlier in the day, the agent had tried to impress us with its location. 'Just a tick.' He hurried up a grade to the corner. At the end of the street, he climbed onto a brick pillar and pointed his patent leather shoes and onyx ring due east. He shouted back, 'You can see the ocean from here.'

My husband reassured me. 'It's only for two years, sweetheart, then we can go back.'

Wives followed their husbands. I'd recently been offered twelve months' training as deputy to replace the one who planned to retire in twelve months' time. I'd already been given some of her part-time position, teaching art and craft, and had been given an additional day for drama from K to 6; a dream job for me.

The previous year, I'd written a play called *Boy for Sale*. I'd obtained permission to use the songs from the musical *Oliver*. It was a whole-school production. Actors were my sixth graders and the rest of school was the choir. The mistress-in-charge requested that the barmaid scene, and any related violence, be excluded, so I invented another Betty who met the requirements and refinements of a ladies' college, not quite Dickens territory. The satisfaction of seeing the written word come to life on stage was always exciting, and here was another play which represented another small step in my writing life, not that I knew that's what I was doing.

When I announced that my husband was being transferred to Newcastle, it meant handing in my resignation.

Miss P sat me down and closed the office door. 'If, as you say, it's only for two years, can he go and come back on weekends? It seems such a shame to –'

It was certainly an option which I hadn't considered. It also made common sense. We were in the middle of making house plans. It would take at least twelve to eighteen months to complete. We had trailed around project home villages for months. We'd looked at Jennings homes and the like, and had settled on a cute Cape Cod design which would fit snugly at the end of the cul-de-sac. We'd already decided on kitchen and bathroom colours: white with navy blue trim.

The current deputy offered another option. She would put off her retirement for another year or two if that helped. This was a generous offer considering she was a gifted portrait artist who was looking forward to painting full-time; her new painting studio had just been finished. It would be an interim arrangement and was definitely something to discuss.

We moved to Newcastle. After some months, I reported back to the mistress-in-charge that the schedules clerk was to be given another promotion in Newcastle and added that we hoped to start a family soon, thanked her for the opportunity and reluctantly declined. I knew there was another eager contender waiting in the wings.

Boy for Sale, 'Ingleholem', PLC, 1972.

'Ingleholme', Pymble Ladies' College.

43
Pumpkin Dreams

No. 7 had a bright, floral, three-tiered display. It was a landscaped garden from which I made dozens of posies. There were posies for new-found friends, posies for the sick and dying and posies for the abundance of new babies in the Crescent. At one stage, Happy Nappy Valley numbered seventy-four children under sixteen.

In a very large brandy balloon, a gift from one of my students, I created miniature floral gardens from roses, fuchsias and alyssum. It sat on the glass top of a round coffee table in the living room. When I knelt on the floor and stared up into the balloon, I could see layers of refraction. It was sheer beauty and an entirely different perspective to the actual.

We lived in a hollow, tight-hugging valley. Bellbirds sang in the reserve out the back. We knew that developers had bought what we called the Reserve but had no idea when building would take place. One day after work, I drove down our side driveway and heard bulldozers and saw that grand eucalypts, which had lined the other side of our back fence, had gone. I stood up on the back veranda and looked due north and saw a barren stretch of land beyond our boundary. It had taken only a few hours to destroy. The bleeding gums lay dispossessed. Without dignity. Displaced elderly. Their compliance was frightening. Bird calls were replaced by discordant bulldozers, screaming saws and the eventual roar of lawnmowers and edge cutters. In spite of the brick jungle which mushroomed out the back, stars still shone brighter than all the new porch lights.

Meanwhile, I undertook fertility tests. I kept daily temperature charts and we conscientiously undertook the schedule as required. But to no avail. We decided to apply for adoption through the Uniting Church. We travelled to Sydney for the necessary interviews and waited.

A few months after the first appointment, I fell pregnant. I rang the adoption agency. The social worker suggested we wait before taking our name off the list. I didn't like the sound of that. It suggested something untoward. I knew God wouldn't let that happen.

I dream of pumpkins. A vivid dream. A lush vine in the backyard. It grows thick with lush, dewy leaves. Everything is king-size, blowing, dancing in the breeze. Golden flowers gleam. Leaves circle. Tight. tighter. Flowers drop. Leaves shrivel. A ring of stinking mush.

A few days later, spotting started. No pain. I was meant to sing a small solo in church that morning but it was like something ripped inside me in the lower abdomen. I said to the tenor, 'Can't sing today… can't go.'

'You have to.'

'I know.'

When we arrived at church, one of the older members of the choir came and said, 'By the looks of you, you shouldn't be here.'

Excused from choir, I sat with the congregation. Shivering started and more pain; wet pain. When we got home, I rang my mother.

'I've never had anything like it so I'm not too sure – put your legs up.'

'I have an appointment tomorrow with the specialist. The results might explain –'

'Here's hoping… Make sure you rest.'

I went to bed, propped up feet, stayed still and prayed for relief from this combination of pain and bleeding. By now I was sixteen weeks, busy knitting baby's clothes and preparing the nursery. Because I'd passed the three months mark, I'd started to tell people our exciting news. The intermittent spotting of the past few weeks was unsettling but the obstetrician had said it was quite common and nothing to worry about. He organised tests.

Next morning, as usual, I drove G to the bus stop which was just around the corner then headed for the local GP, who rang the obstetrician. He said for me to go to hospital. He'd contact them and he'd call in and see me sometime during the day. The GP offered to organise an ambulance for me but I had the cat and dog to feed and a bag to pack.

'As long as you go straight home then straight to hospital.'

My intention was to do things as calmly as possible, not panic, do things in their right order and the pain might even go away and the bleeding might stop. Order might be restored. Anything was possible.

I rang G to see if he could take me but they told me he was 'in conference', so my neighbour and good friend said she'd drive me but would I mind just popping along to her place while she got ready. It was only two doors down.

'Come in...haven't had my shower yet...won't be long.'

I sat on a high stool in the kitchen and waited. The short walk, carrying a small bag, had exacerbated the situation. The generous Earth Mother of Four had never experienced a miscarriage and neither had I, so we didn't really understand.

Soon J came out of the shower drying her hair. 'I'll put a wash on first. Would you like a cuppa? I'm going to need one.'

'No, thanks. I really need to get to hospital. They're expecting me. If you don't mind, can I use your phone? I think I'll ring for an ambulance.'

'No, no. I'm almost ready.' She made her cuppa and sorted out the weekly washing. She separated the coloureds from the whites and put on a load of whitewashing before we headed for Emergency at the Mater Hospital, Waratah.

I thanked my friend for bringing me as they whisked me off in a wheelchair and installed me in a dark single room on a firm, cold bed.

'The doctor should be here soon. Meantime, rest up.'

When Dr C saw me later that day, he said, 'I'm going to admit you to keep the neighbours happy. They can't say that we didn't look after you.'

He and Sister shared knowing looks.

'I was going to see you today to get my test results. Did they show anything?'

He patted my knee. 'You're in good hands. Let's wait and see.'

I clung to hope as he and Sister left the room in whispers. What I didn't know, and what he could have, and should have, told me then was that the results showed the foetus wasn't developing normally and unknown to me he'd already written on my chart 'inevitable abortion'. The good Catholic doctor had handed me over to Mother Nature, who worked hard for two days. The situation deteriorated to such a stage I haemorrhaged and shook uncontrollably. I fell into shock. I believed I heard another woman screaming. I knew exactly how she felt. I sent her one of my incomprehensible prayers.

I asked Sister what was wrong with her.

She held my hand and said, 'There's no one, darling.'

Was I on another planet?

Then Love comes and stands beside me. Tall. Warm. Radiant. I turn my head. Can almost touch a loving presence. It's right there. Is it Jesus' love? That's who I think it is. I know the nuns are praying for me and know first-hand the power of prayer. Love is standing there, answering prayer. It's overwhelmingly comforting.

A visibly distressed Sister started patting my hand faster. 'Doctor is on his way…difficult to get hold of.'

Dr C arrived and saw the extent of Mother Nature's efforts. He winced and apologised. In a matter of minutes, there was a needle and no more pain. The other woman stopped crying, too. The Sisters wrapped me in extra blankets. By the time the middle-aged, balding porter arrived, I was subdued, thankful for pain relief.

He jollied me as he wheeled me to the lift. Once inside the lift he said, 'And what are you up to tonight, love?'

'I'm losing my baby.'

'Oh, love, I'm really sorry.'

'You weren't to know.'

The mother-to-be in me had to face reality. It was the porter who unwittingly helped me say it out loud. As we ascended, I knew I was leaving dreams and hopes behind. I stared at the thermal white blankets that covered me. It all seemed so clinical. So Life and Death were white.

When I was wheeled into the theatre, Dr C and his team gathered around, all the while chatting, smiling, chatting, smiling. They lifted me up and across onto the chilly, narrow bed. I tried to smile but life was too raw. They were cheery. Was it themselves they were cheering? It certainly wasn't me. Their camaraderie felt inappropriate. I needed recognition, reverence from them for the loss of a little life.

There were no words to hold back the incoming tide of grief. I didn't want to hear about the specialist's golf scores as I went under, his round face telling me it was dinnertime and he was looking forward to going home, having curried sausages. The aroma of his disrespect was still there when I woke. My bud and I deserved better.

The next day, I counted my blessings as I packed to go home. I was one of the lucky ones, privileged to have been born in a time and place with access to life-saving medical intervention. Yes, I was wheeled out of hospital with a devastatingly empty womb, aching breasts and confused hormones but I could be thankful for my life. There were women in less fortunate circumstances who lost both.

I had a follow-up consultation with the obstetrician six weeks later. I sat opposite him as he cut and pasted notes about my recent loss into a manilla folder.

'It proves one thing,' he said. 'You'll never have any trouble carrying full term. I'm surprised it held on for so long.' He leant back in his chair. Casual. Still no eye contact. 'If you hadn't lost it then, you would have to have carried it to full-term.'

Couldn't he understand I held onto it for so long because I didn't want to lose my baby. 'Was it a boy or a girl?'

'A boy.'

'What went wrong?'

'Not developing properly. Quite common.'

Still no eye contact, no commiserations. The specialist continued to read and write notes as if he was catching up on my case. Then more cutting, more pasting. I wondered when we'd talk about what actually happened.

'When I first went into hospital, did you expect that to happen?'

The sound of scissors faltered.

'I mean, did you know that I was going to miscarry?'

'Abort? Yes.'

The unseen lioness in me began to prowl his desk. I was looking for blood I once shed. 'So why was I allowed to go to the point of haemorrhage? Why did I have to go through –? I mean, I ended up losing my baby in pieces. It was, was –' There were no words. Anyway, lionesses don't usually speak in sentences.

'It was a mass. A lump, flesh. It was never going to –'

Still no eye contact. He put his scissors down and prepared to stand, indicating the consultation was over. I remained seated. The hair on my lioness's back was standing on end. Indignation and determination anchored me to the chair.

'As you know,' I said, stunned at the strength of my growl, 'I had unbelievable pain, shock. I'd never want anyone to suffer that. I'd like to know, if you already knew, why wasn't I given a curette? It would have saved –'

Dr C stood back as if someone's claws were drawing blood.

I continued, 'Why didn't I have a curette straight away?'

He still didn't look at me or answer. He shuffled papers on his desk. This short, bantam-like man was obviously answerable only to himself. He strode to the door and opened it. 'It's too complicated to explain.'

I wanted to say, you could at least try. I rose and, in an instant, he was no longer prey. I wanted to get out of the room, away from the disgust standing at the door. I nodded as I walked past, an acknowledgement to myself that I'd never see him again. In essence, he'd curried favour with his dogma, at the expense of –.

The next gynaecologist the GP recommended put me on hormone treatment for twelve months. And, for the first time in years and years, I felt strong and well.

The first Sunday after my loss, my husband and I were walking out of church. I didn't feel like speaking to anyone, so hurried to the car. I couldn't bear to face any sympathy from the few who knew. We hurried to the car when I heard shouting.

'Anne, Anne, wait, wait.' It was the woman who helped me lead the girls' group. She raced up the last step of the steep path puffing.

I felt ashamed of my wish to avoid her. Here she was going to so much trouble to see me.

She grabbed both my hands and kissed me on both cheeks. 'Terrible, terrible…but I want to share something with you. God has laid it heavy on my heart. I know why you lost your baby. I feel led to tell you. You lost it because you're not right with the Lord.'

'Really?' I said in a controlled monotone as if speaking from some subterranean level of disbelief. I sent it back to her. 'I suppose that all those billions of unbelievers, who breed like rabbits, are right with the Lord?'

'Oh, they don't count.'

Unfortunately, she believed it. I took my hands back, shook my head and climbed into the car. I started to count aloud one, two, three, four. G had been waiting in the car and hadn't heard. 'Get me out of here before I explode.' Here was another one currying favour with some fundamental dogma at the expense of fundamental compassion.

I didn't need spiritual guidance. I'd felt the presence of the Lord, of a higher being of Love with me in hospital. It was like I received a holy hug, powered by strong arms of prayer. The overwhelming warmth of spirit was stronger and more real than me or the kind sisters who prayed so faithfully beside my bed.

Once back home, I found I couldn't share my loss. If I mentioned it to G, he'd say, 'Put it out of your mind, sweetheart. It's not going to help if you keep thinking about it.'

'Would you mind if we named him John? It's your middle name and your father's name.'

'Okay.'

I snuggled up to him while he read one of his model train magazines. I needed to keep warm. I always felt cold these days.

When talking to Ruby about it on the phone, she'd stop me. 'Look, let it go. There's nothing you can do about it now. It won't do you any good thinking about it. I don't understand. I never had an ounce of trouble. Try and think of something else.'

One day, shortly after coming home from hospital, I was hanging out the washing.

My neighbour, who'd had a miscarriage earlier in the year, called out over the fence, 'How are you going? I was a mess when it happened to me. I cried for days. Had to go and stay at Mum's.'

So she'd cried too. At least someone understood. I'd felt ashamed of crying all the time but made sure it was when I was alone: when making the bed, washing up, driving the car. I was so grateful to my neighbour for having shared.

44

The First Smile

When I came out of the Mater Hospital, I confirmed with the adoption agency that our earlier application was still current. I returned to casual teaching and waited for a call. It came mid-October.

The nineteen-year-old biological mother had been sent to Sydney to work in a special hostel for unmarried mothers before giving birth. She was from Queensland, a solicitor's clerk. The father, ten years older, had studied veterinary science in New Zealand for four years before coming to Australia to be a jackaroo. We were told we were the most suitable match and that his mother was reluctant to sign release papers. We were told the young baby was no longer in hospital but with a foster-mother.

We waited the necessary thirty days in case his mother changed her mind. Or so we were told. What to believe? Today, so much more is known about the traumas unmarried mothers experienced and how so many were forced to give up their baby.

The timing of Paul's arrival was fortuitous. In recent weeks I'd been waking up with aching breasts. The body had a memory and, had I not miscarried, it would've been close to full term. Before his arrival, whenever I saw a newborn, I hardly trusted myself to be near them for fear of breaking down. Seeing a young mother pushing a pram as I drove along the road was enough to start me weeping. On rainy days, I needed wipers more for my eyes than the windscreen.

When I met the foster-mother on handover day, she told me she had four boisterous boys of her own. 'He doesn't like noise – hasn't smiled yet – intense – jumpy – fingers still clenched. What are you going to call him?'

'Either Paul or David. I think he looks more like Paul.'

'I agree.' She smiled and handed me the baby clinic card. 'We'd given him a name. I shouldn't have crossed it out.'

The baby clinic card showed Paul had been attending the same baby health clinic I'd attended as a child. I changed his nappy, talking to him all the while and he didn't take his eyes off me.

The foster-mother said, 'Look, he's forgotten me already.'

Was he listening for a particular voice, for the one he'd heard in the womb? Did I sound similar? Would he always search? There was such an intensity and anxiety in his clenched fingers. Sharp, loud noises startled him. I held him close, closer. I reassured him with hugs and kisses and sang lullabies.

It's a very long week until our young son smiles. He is six weeks old. His first smile is engraved on my heart. He's having an early-morning sunbath on our gauzed-in back veranda. He looks up and smiles at the bright red geranium close by. It's hanging in a basket beside his bassinet. I'm so excited. For the first time, his fingers unfurl. I kiss his open palms.

I think of his biological mother. Did she ever hold these perfect little fingers? Did they ever curl up around her finger like they are now curling around mine? Tears fall. I can't imagine her pain. I'm only months from my recent loss. My grief weeps with hers. How much greater hers would be! I pray for the nineteen-year-old young woman who would've walked out of hospital with empty arms. I knew what that black hole felt like. I gave thanks for the miracle she'd given us. Joy cupped loss.

The hardest adjustment was suddenly to be at home, full-time, answerable to another clock. This timetable was far removed from bells and books. This little person's o'clock was nothing like keeping a class full of active students on-task and on time. This was harder. The new timetable felt upside down. It was nocturnally driven. In spite of the early efforts to change the routine, most feeding took place at night. Sleep an hour. Feed an hour. Sleep an hour. Feed an hour. It took three months to rearrange the feeding schedule. I could hardly see through the grey veil of exhaustion.

Anne and Graeme with Paul, 1974.

I bottle-fed him against my bare breast. Adoptive mothers were advised to do that. It helped bond, they said, and it did. It also gave the newborn a heartbeat to listen to, to be soothed by. My body was ripe for this miracle of life lying so peacefully in my arms. My hormones had been hungry for baby. Blessedly, Paul arrived in the same week our biological son was due to be born. My hormones were happy now.

The adoption agency had stipulated we tell our son at the earliest opportunity that he was adopted. That day came much earlier than expected. I could not, and would not, dodge it. It had to be done. If not now, when?

Paul was about three-and-a-half years old, the same age he was when he asked me if God made the trees, then who made God. We were driving in the car and he was sitting in the back on his booster seat. 'Mummy, I know why I have a round head. Because you have a round tummy. G has a square head because Auntie J has a square tummy. You have a round tummy.'

We were sitting at traffic lights. 'Darling, you were born in another lovely mummy's tummy.'

'No.' And he repeated his reasoning.

My toddler and I made fresh mud scones and cooked them in the sun oven. Under the Japanese willow, we sat on rugs and looked up into the sky and watched clouds make pictures and tell stories. In summer, under the weeping willows, we waded in the baby's pool. In autumn, we swept up golden carpets of willow leaves with our bare hands.

Now a full-time mother at home, I began to meet my Happy Nappy neighbours. It was fortunate that five of us in a row, on the low side of the street, were 'transfers'. Our families were too far away to offer any regular support, so we built a strong support system. We shared backyards, endless cups of tea and jam and Vegemite sandwiches. On rainy days, everyone came to our place and sheltered in our indoor/outdoor patio. Children moulded sweaty home-made play dough, spilt drinks and built tall towers out of blocks of wood.

Gardening, always a passion, was less and less so. Very little time was spent out the front. The blue couch dominated the tiered garden and G had a solution. It was something he'd been wanting to do: dismantle the beds.

'But the flowers are surviving.'

Tiers of roses, strawberries, alyssum, daisies and the like were removed and the area graded. Pencil pines were installed, symmetrically, on either side of the driveway in the exact centre of newly installed rock and cactus garden beds at the top of the driveway.

One afternoon, G set out to plant some more pencil pines, this time in front of the house on the lawn. I was asked to stand in one particular spot and hold the other end of the tape measure. He was very particular about symmetry. I knew that.

Even so, I moved a little to one side, weighing up the balance of shape and line. 'Over here feels quite good.'

Le Measurer threw the tape onto the ground and disappeared down our steep driveway. His sense of high drama was mostly entertaining but not this time. It was obvious his wife would not, could not stand still even when told to.

I blinkered my eyes more and more. I imagined the lost tiers of flowers in my mind's eye.

Another miscarriage. More weight loss. Shadow weight. Empty womb. I'd come home from shopping, too weak to carry the endless bags of groceries up our steep stairs. I'd put one leg after the other and be tempted to complain. But how could I when I knew there were hungry people around who had little money to buy groceries. My husband was sick of me being sick and I was sick of me, too.

A neighbour, who was a local, with a lot of family support, expressed her frustration with me one day when I was unwell and had to cancel an arrangement we'd made for me to babysit her son. 'He may find someone else, you know. A man can't be blamed for wandering if, you know.'

No, I didn't know. I just knew I hardly was. And, apart from the agony and ecstasy of raising an active son, and our family grass presented well-manicured and green, these days it always seemed like winter in my garden.

45
The Wings of a Dove

When Paul was about two years old, a teaching colleague was studying part-time at Newcastle University. At this stage, I'd been a full-time mother for two years. 'Why don't you try it?'

'I'd love to but I don't have a scholarship and I can't afford the fees.'

'No university fees... Whitlam...'

'Does that mean that I –?

My first lecture in English 1 at the University of Newcastle brought back a vivid memory: the physics lecture at NSW uni. The music this time was not on the board. It was in the language, in the subtext, the Word. Here was soul food.

But there was a struggle. Husband was visibly upset when, one night a week, his wife headed off to uni. We'd agreed that, for this one night during term time, he would be there to look after our son between 5.30 and 9.30. The schedules clerk always arrived home and changed over at 5.48 p.m. He'd calculated that it would take twelve minutes to drive there. I reminded him that his wife was not a bus and didn't need to account for running times between bus stops but to no avail.

To relieve further stress which occurred on these nights, such as coming home and going in to kiss Paul goodnight and finding, two weeks in a row, that he was still catching his crying-breath in his sleep, I determined to change babysitting arrangements. No lecture was worth this. Daytime lectures and tutorials were arranged.

By 1976 there was a ground swell of change and activism. On the agenda was the issue of homosexuality, which wouldn't be decriminalised in NSW until 1984. There was Germaine Greer and *The*

Female Eunuch continuing to challenge women's roles in a provocative, witty way. There was change on the home front, too. I'd enrolled in university part-time and had taken up painting, bought my own kiln and started painting on fine porcelain. My health improved but as I grew stronger and more lively it unsettled my husband.

Edith Schaeffer, unknowingly, became my mentor at this time. Her book *Hidden Art* held me tight in my search to create a more loving home. It taught me how to create simple beauty in the home and be Love itself for the family. I almost knew each chapter off by heart. I'd been searching for support. Although there was positive change in the home on some levels, at a more fundamental level I'd learnt to live with grief: grief for the loss of a relationship that never grew, grief for our lack of intimacy. I can't remember its name but, at the same time, there was another significant book I read, about a woman who'd been widowed when her children were young. I seemed to have a lot in common with her. While my spouse hadn't died, I grieved my loss of him.

We walk into a crowded gardening expo.

My eyes dart everywhere. I see something. 'Look,' I say to my husband, but he doesn't hear.

He's distracted. What can be so distracting? Two tall, very handsome young men, in short shorts, discuss an exhibit. My husband is transfixed. The floor tilts; almost trips me into a nearby exhibit. No one sees the hurtling missing pieces fall into heart-thumping place as we walk and talk, hand in hand, husband and wife.

I dreamt of moving, constantly. For twelve months in my dreams there was a backyard with succulent vines, spring blossoms, magnolias, azaleas, terracotta pavers. Birds sunned themselves on nearby wooden window sills. There was the smell of salt water.

'Do you know if or when we'll be transferring back to Sydney?'

'Difficult to say.'

We'd agreed to move upmarket to keep in touch with Sydney prices, for the anticipated return. It'd been a long two years. In the meantime, I found an architect-designed brown-brick, blue-tiled house, with spring blossoms, azaleas, terracotta pavers and birds sunning themselves on warm wooden windowsills on the other side of our hill. The smell of saltwater was as exciting as the sight of bushland and beyond; the grand sweep of Pacific Ocean seen from the family-sized front veranda.

Packing was physically exhausting. I fell into bed each night beyond exhaustion. I was woken in the middle of the night one night and wondered why. That's when I saw a strong presence at the foot of our bed. I looked at it. It was misty, life-like-light. It exuded overwhelming calm. Love flooded my body. Stilled my mind. In that moment, regardless of what I worried might be ahead, I knew all would be well.

We moved over the hill not far away. This time we were on the high side of the street where grass was just as green. The house faced due east. It looked out over the bush, out to Glenrock Lagoon and to the Pacific Ocean. Soon we'd be watching the sunrise or the moon set on the ocean's still waters. It always looked so peaceful out there.

My young son and I were observing its beauty one night when he said, 'Mummy, can one of Daddy's friends come here every night? He's nice then.'

'Great idea, darling.' I ached for my young son, who wasn't afraid to speak out from his little four-year-old's perspective. Those few words altered me. It was clear. We were all suffering.

Sometimes, it was easier not to feel. In fact, my feelings became so blinkered it was easier to say, 'I think...' and I seemed to lose the ability to say 'I feel.' If I'd been asked what I felt, I wouldn't have been able to say. But, in spite of internal family issues, we did have happy times. We sang in the church choir on Sundays. We shared a rich fellowship with friends, family, neighbours. We also sang in a small group, the Cathedral Singers. It was led by the dynamic M. Dudman, organist at Newcastle Cathedral at the time. We sang at the completion of the tower of Christchurch Cathedral in 1979.

At that time, I, too, was preparing for a momentous occasion. It was still too early to announce, considering my history. During the service, I felt a gripping low pelvic pain which was as discordant as the contemporary music we were singing. Next day I was admitted to hospital. Miscarriage at eight weeks. Another curette. Another grief.

Other fronts were more productive. I wrote a couple of programmes for the Hunter Churches' Media Commission. They were produced by NBN 3. We sang in Newcastle City Hall, for a Musica Viva concert. It was also recorded for ABC radio. I sang the solo in the Easter Hymn, 'Oh, rejoice for the Lord has arisen,' from *Cavalleria Rusticana*, by Mascagni. Before the concert, I lost a couple of kilos with worry. I wasn't a performer, always preferred producing.

Singing in choirs, surrounded by spine-tingling harmony, was vibrational life support. We sang as one. We were all feathers of the same bird. We could soar together on the wings of a dove. We took flight on Mendelssohn's 'Hear my Prayer'.

> 'Oh, for the wings, for the wings of a dove,
> far away, far away would I roam…
> In the wilderness build me a nest
> and remain there for ever at rest…
> i-in the wilderness, build me a ne-est…'

Soon after we moved into 35 Valaud Crescent, Highfields, I was very sick from exhaustion and gastro when the Presence woke me again. This time it was close to me, right beside me. It was Love more luminous. I fell into a deep sleep in the knowledge that Love and Light were aware.

There didn't seem to be any reason for my severe vertigo attacks. I'd had tests which did reveal something important but it had nothing to do with vertigo. Apparently, when I slept I was burning as many calories as one would be expected to burn in an active day. It was something to do with anabolism over catabolism or was it the other way round? In other words, this very small eater, who had a lifelong swallowing problem, needed more fuel to get ahead of the metabolic rate.

Over twelve months, a dietician helped me reach my goal weight, eight stone, and I felt stronger. I kept my busy schedule with family, friends, tutoring, painting, church, singing and I increased body speed.

It was an excellent way of sublimating unexpressed feelings of betrayal. I felt trapped for life. Vows had been taken. For better, for worse. We didn't divorce.

I attended counselling sessions with psychologist TT; my necessary Angel. I could unload. At times, I hinted about my situation to Ruby, but, as she said, marriage was more give than take. And I agreed with her and could understand why she would say that. Over the years, she and Stan stood united. They both gave more than they took.

The diagnostic physician said, 'I'm worried about your blood pressure. It's getting higher. Are there things to resolve?'

I nodded. 'It's impossible. If I tried, it's not worth –'

I was afraid of any desperate action. As it was, I had to leap over my pride; my big sense of failure. On the other hand, I was very fortunate. I had strong relationships with family, friends and neighbours. It was the dichotomy that existed between home life and the rest; a disconnect.

TT said, 'Compassion is a great strength for you to have but in the wrong hands your strengths can become your weaknesses.'

Dr F said, 'You'd be much better off out of that situation, you know.'

What did he know? How much did he know and from whom? This was embarrassing. Our GP was a parishioner and attended the same church. I sat in his surgery looking at him while he challenged me to change what I could. Stared past him through the open Venetians. Focused on the healthy sasanqua camellia outside this sunny, north-facing window. Shrugged. Looked back. To remove the concern on Dr F's face, I assured him I'd think about it. He made a note.

Late that afternoon when watering the garden, I thought about it. I watered the azaleas, the magnolia, the tree ferns, the irises, the daisies and thought about it. How could I leave all this? I knelt down and pulled out persistent weeds around the jonquils and freesias. As I did so, there seemed to be a loud chorus behind me. 'Can't leave this, you silly girl.' I messaged to myself, try harder, be a better wife. No other option even though our marriage was a train wreck on an abandoned line.

46

Lateral Thinking

Paul started at the local infants' school in 1980. It was in walking distance from home.

I drove around the corner one morning when I saw a young child in the playground attempting to climb the very high crossbar which held the structure together. It was never meant to be climbed. I slowed down. If the child fell, he'd fall onto hard earth. What should I do? Who was supervising the child?

I got out of the car and looked closer. It was Paul. Of course. He had feet like a gecko. In preschool he was the first to scale the brand-new safety fence on its first day to fetch the big ball which had bounced over the fence and rolled away down the road.

Paul waved to me from the high bar when he saw me coming. Had he gone to the toilet and taken a circuitous route back to class?

The teacher said he'd been sent out to play, 'Because he learns too quickly.'

'Is that a problem?'

'Yes.' She listed kindergarten outcomes. 'He needs to learn to sit still and wait and not call out answers. It's all part of his socialisation. He has to know how to tie his own shoelaces' – good luck with that – 'and count to twenty and know how to put his things away.'

I was underwhelmed. 'Do you think you could set him an individual programme?' I asked, because all teachers face differences in both ability and application in any classroom. At this stage, I hadn't mentioned I was a primary school teacher who'd once had to prepare fifteen different programmes for one particular class.

'No. He simply has to learn to sit still on the mat and wait until the others have learnt their words. Another problem is he gives the answers to his friends if they don't know them.'

That sounded very naughty. No wonder he was regularly sent outside into the playground to play, unsupervised.

I requested a parent/teacher interview and came away with a handful of facts. I headed into town, into the grammar school, to see if there were any vacancies. I knew the independent system well. I enjoyed working in them but private education was not our preference. At this stage, though, it was critical that our lateral thinking, free-wheeling son had a more challenging, stimulating environment.

Soon the young student was complaining. 'It's not fair. At this school I'm not allowed to go out and see the sun. We have to sit in the dark and work all day.'

Paul David.

47
CVA

During the previous twelve months, I'd been sent to a diagnostic physician because of disabling bouts of vertigo. There didn't seem to be any explanation. After each attack, my left side was weak and I couldn't walk a straight line. It was like I needed a realignment.

I was thirty-seven, busy-busy and, although I felt stronger with the weight gain, I had claps of thunder in my head more than usual. When it happened, I'd look around to see if anyone else heard. Clusters of migraines rolled in and out, one after the other, for almost four months. That year, I withdrew from part-time studies.

G and I now lived worlds apart but, publicly, we walked hand-in-hand, your very own Mr and Mrs Brady; the classic couple front.

The night I took my first blood pressure tablet, I fell into a sound sleep. At one stage, I stirred and tried to turn over but couldn't. I seemed glued to the bed. I remembered the tablets. This was probably a side effect and with that I fell asleep.

The previous day I'd had a routine check-up with the diagnostic physician. He was satisfied my weight problem had been resolved. I understood the effects of a fast metabolic rate now and knew how to maintain weight. But the riddle of vertigo attacks hadn't been solved.

The physician's most pressing concern was with my blood pressure. 'Your blood pressure's been too high for too long.'

Next morning I sat at the painting table facing the southern window. It was overcast and the glare in the window was unusually blinding and I had trouble focusing. I felt disconnected from my surroundings. What was happening? I walked slowly to the kitchen, slower than usual, trying to calm myself down. I could only wade back to the room as if through quicksand.

Later in the day, I stumbled as I prepared the evening meal. 'Dinner's ready.' I turned to take the plates to the table but my left leg wouldn't move. I tried again. I put the plates down and put my hands on my hips. What was going on? Then I realised I couldn't feel my left hip. Pins and needles up and down the left side. I tried to lift my left foot. Numbness was spreading at the same pace as my panic. I said to Paul, 'Get your father quickly, please.'

In the meantime, I tried to reach the phone but couldn't.

G called out, 'I'm watching the news.'

I called back, 'I'm the news right now. Can you come here quickly, please. I need a doctor.'

It was after hours and in hindsight we should've called an ambulance, but who would've thought it was serious? There was no pain, just an increasing numbness and pins and needles down one side. Without pain it couldn't be serious, could it?

The call centre operator asked, 'Is she in pain?'

While we waited for someone to come, Paul raced in and got Big Ted and he and Big Ted hopped up into the bed with me and didn't leave my side.

After an hour's wait, Graeme rang the after hours number again. I suggested he say I was in pain. Soon a young locum arrived and examined me. I needed to go to hospital. He filled out a form and gave it to my husband to hand in at reception. Out of earshot the doctor told GB his prognosis; a cerebrovascular accident (CVA).

Instead of an ambulance, my husband wanted to take me to hospital. It was with some difficulty that we made our way down the internal stairs because it was as if my left side had stayed behind on the bed. I was surprised when I couldn't sign the admission form. My left hand just wasn't there. I could see it was there but, at the same time, it wasn't. Judging by the careful and controlled actions of nursing staff, I knew this was serious.

Our son stayed with neighbours that night and I lay in a hospital bed in a small room, waiting for a neurologist to come and see me. After an hour, and with no neurologist in sight, my husband said he had better leave because it was getting late and he had to go to work next day.

'Could you take tomorrow off?' I really needed a hand to hold or, at least, someone who could distract me.

'Sweetheart, we're flat out. You'll be right. Nothing to worry about. Make sure you rest.'

I wanted to retort that resting wouldn't be too hard because, if you really looked at me, you'd see I couldn't get out of bed by myself and go anywhere. After he left, I stared at, but couldn't really see, a painting hanging on the wall. It became my focus, my support.

It was unusually quiet in my head. I listened. Was I fading away? Was this how death arrived? Did it just creep in, unannounced, without bothering to check in at the front desk? If so, there'd certainly be no raging 'against the dying of the light'. Was I slipping 'into that good night'?

When the neurologist arrived, it was late. Thursday night. We recognised each other. We sang in the same special interest choir.

'You have a history of migraine, don't you? Nothing to worry about…it'll pass…temporary paralysis from migraine.'

The next day, I caught a subtle frown on the junior neurologist's face when they were conducting tests. He remarked that my left eye's response was… A CAT scan might be necessary…

T took another look. 'No hurry. We'll pop her in for a CAT scan on Monday.'

It was Friday and I was to stay in emergency until then.

'But don't worry,' T said, 'I'm confident you'll be out of here before then.'

After they left, an older woman in the bed opposite me came over and sat in the chair beside me. 'What's happening?' Although she would've heard every word.

'Cat scan Monday…thinks it's a migraine.'

The retired matron leant forward in the chair and whispered, 'I think you've had a stroke but I'm not a doctor…'

That certainly put up my heart rate and she had to be wrong. She wasn't a doctor. I couldn't have had a stroke. I'd seen lots of stroke patients when we used to visit Gran in the nursing home. Stroke patients were bedridden for years. And they were old. I was thirty-seven.

The resident and his assistant continued to conduct regular tests and we could all see there was a deterioration even so I was kept in emergency for three days.

Monday morning. Cat scan. Unexpectedly, I was moved to a ward, fortuitously in a bed opposite my new-found matron friend.

Monday afternoon. A visit by the head neurologist and his assistants. Before T spoke, he looked as though he was praying, hands held together, praying-mantis-style.

I said, 'I don't like the look of this.'

'I'm so sorry, Anne. You've had a cerebral haemorrhage.'

'A ce-re-what?'

'A bleed in the brain.'

'A stroke?'

'As things go, it's a relatively mild one. I apologise. It's your history of migraine that –'

By this time I was completely paralysed down my left side, from my toes up to my neck. I could talk but words came slowly, while some disappeared altogether, but I kept searching for them and found them again months later. By now, I didn't like more than one person speaking at a time and I could put a pin in the middle of my chest and find the fine line between nothingness and fullness.

'You've got youth on your side…veins in very good condition. That's what saved you.'

'Do you think it had anything to do with the new blood pressure tablets. Could they have –?'

'No. You were lucky to be on them. It'll be months now before we know what caused it. We have to wait for the blood to dissolve.'

'What happens now?'

'I'll send you home in a week or two. We've had a meeting and decided you're too young to go to a convalescent home. It'd be detrimental. You can go home with provisos, when you're independent enough to go to and from the bathroom…'

What a marvellous goal! Who'd have thought that getting to and from the loo would, one day, become the sole purpose of my day and my ticket to freedom.

Later that afternoon, another patient was moved into our ward. M had been playing pennants golf earlier in the day and had suffered a major stroke. It was going to be a tough recovery for her and she'd need every bit of competitive spirit to overcome the major obstacles on her next green.

The elderly patient on my right was happily packing. She was looking forward to going home in the morning, so it was a surprise when in the early hours of the morning I heard the nurse gently call her name. Curtains were drawn and soon there was a quiet busyness around her bed. We were now in the dress circle of Life and Death. It was peaceful. Quiet. I was so impressed by the staff's response. So reverential. Such respect and dignity.

This wasn't the first time I'd experienced death in the bed next to me.

48

A Solitary Nature

I'm twelve years old. I'm in the children's ward at the Mater Misceracordia Hospital, Wollstonecraft. I've just had my adenoids and tonsils removed. My sister is in a bed further down the ward, having had the same operation. A young girl is in the bed next to me. She's about eight years old. Her arms and parts of her body are bandaged. When the nurses come to do things with her bandages, the little girl screams. She whimpers all night and all day. One day she calls out and sobs for her mummy. They tell her she has to wait until visiting hours, then she can see her mummy.

It's the middle of the night and Doctor and Sister stand by her bed. She's been whimpering for hours but now has stopped.

Curtains are drawn. There's a lot of whispering then the little girl's mummy and daddy arrive. They cry and cry. I want to cry.

A nurse comes over and tells me everything's all right. 'You roll over and go to sleep.'

In the morning, I can't stop looking at the empty bed. They're disinfecting it. Soon the bed has fresh sheets. It doesn't seem right. We mustn't forget the little girl. It's her bed. The nurses try to cheer me as I sit on the side of my bed and think about the little girl.

At first, I don't understand but then I see nurses commiserating. They look sad. I know then the little girl is dead. I don't want to forget her. Even when I walk around the ward with my sister, because the nurse says we have to talk to the other children, I feel the little girl is walking beside us. In my imagination, she's in a blue dress.

It's a big surprise when Ruby arrives. It's early in the day. It's not visiting hours but we're told we can go home now, right now. On the way home, I ask my parents where they think the little girl is. No, not her body. Where is she? Where is she, the person of she?'

I never forgot the little girl, and here I was again, in a hospital bed, wondering where my neighbour's person had gone. Was she the spirit of hush, the feeling of overwhelming peace that filled the room that night? Was it she, now free from mortal body?

After this, death was very much on my mind. The next few days, staff were so attentive I wondered if they expected me to die too. Maybe, maybe not.

When it was time to go home, the neurologist said, 'You can't be too careful.' I was given a list of do's and don'ts. He reiterated, 'Remember the next twelve months are crucial.'

By now, I had a strong, calm certainty. It arrived as a determined voice, accompanied by an image of a person in a bed in a ward. I was told, 'You'll get well, get well, get well.' It sounded so clear that my reaction, at first, was to look to the left to see who was speaking to me. It was only then I realised the voice was within.

Before I left for home, the physiotherapist gave me an instruction. I had to arrange for someone to take me to the hydrotherapy pool twice a week. When there, I was to walk up and down the pool, by the edge, as many times as I could. Start with five minutes then increase to ten. That was my complete rehabilitation programme.

In between my two-hour sleeps, twice a day, I sat in my favourite chair and looked out, counting my blessings. Although the view was unchanged, I'd changed. I was lucky to be alive and was now seeing everything anew. In these early days of recovery, my whole world had shrunk to one room, the sitting room, with its large window framing Glenrock Lagoon, and the lush surrounding bush of Glenrock State Conservation Reserve, a national park, on which my eyes rested before drifting out and seeing the wide silk shantung band of steely blue that was the Pacific Ocean. My world had become whatever was within my reach or what I could see or hear. The telephone was part of that reach.

Rides to and from church occasionally extended the boundaries and news shared by loving visitors was very welcome.

The neurologist had told me there could be no more choral work. I'd miss the fellowship and laughter. I'd miss being part of the glorious, vibrational harmony of the spheres of which we were part. Kind friends lent me books: 'You'll have more time to read now.' But, at this early stage, reading was impossible. Even captions were difficult. For a time, words made little sense. My limit was looking at pictures in the paper and flipping pages of magazines backwards and forwards. The television sounded like utter madness.

In a very automatic, instinctive way, I set up a direct instructional programme and drew up my own rehabilitation programme; an individual programme (IP), in the same way I'd designed many programmes for students with special needs. I had to break down moves into micro moves.

Micro move:
Step one: Sit firmly on chair.
Step two: Lift right knee (the one that works).
Step three: Observe how the foot hangs down when knee is lifted.

Micro move:
Step one: All of the above, then –
Step two: In a sitting position, leave right foot on floor and observe how it sits flat.
Step three: With right hand pull up left leg, using clothing as the pulley.
Step four: Check the angle of left foot, now that the knee is bent, before placing it on floor. (Don't want to twist ankle in the process.)

And so on and on and on. Observe. Observe. Visualise. Visualise until finally, after a couple of months, I was ready to go to hydrotherapy.

This part of my life has its own long story and is too long to be told here. Recovery became purpose and passion. All previous activity was irrelevant, except for anything to do with my young son, who learnt, probably too early for his own good, to be my carer. It was not only my body that had to heal but outlook and attitude as well.

Those first few weeks at home were harsh. I was no longer distracted by the congeniality of hospital mates. My stomach boiled fear. It screamed obscenities on my behalf. It behaved like a recalcitrant ulcer. Six weeks after the CVA, I had a gastroscopy followed by weeks of Gastrogel and Dexsal.

A stroke has a solitary nature. It doesn't want to know you. It and you have to learn to come together. Trying to communicate with the left side of my body was like trying to read invisible instructions on a blank page. I had to write it love letters; build a loving relationship with it and gain its trust. We were in this together and I would not turn my back on it.

Hydrotherapy, once a week, for twelve months helped. Kind friends and neighbours shared the driving to and from the heated pool at Valentine. We even organised a small group to attend a free relaxation course, courtesy of Anne's disability. We were not meant to fall asleep during the exercises but, every week, one of the group always managed to snore their way to the end of the session.

Eventually, I was able to go on small walks. Sometimes, it took weeks to make the next advance. Every advance held its own reward: to the back steps, under the grand old turpentine which sheltered azaleas, camellias, magnolia and ferns, down the back steps, down the sloping path past next door's fish pond and our port wine magnolia, down one, then another step and onto the driveway, down to the gutter, past the three callistemons, observing their growth. Slowly, slowly like the tortoise I became.

Months later, neighbours told me that during those measured months they watched out for me. Apparently, they'd ring one another, some of whom I didn't know. 'She's on her way…keep a lookout.' I had angels watching over me and didn't even know.

I grew stronger and stronger.

My neurologist said, 'Sometimes miracles happen. It's a miracle you survived. You never know, sometimes these things seal themselves off and the blood is rerouted.' The malformation they found in my brain stem was inaccessible, so therefore inoperable. He said, 'The way it bled is what saved you.'

I continued to have the occasional CAT scan, which in turn progressed to MRIs.

After a few years, I read about the possibility of microsurgery whereby previously inoperable malformations can be removed. I enquired about it and was sent to Professor McL in Sydney, who looked at the scans and said, 'You've made such a good recovery, I'd be reluctant…too risky. There's no guarantee you'd be as good as you are now. You most certainly would be left with some permanent damage.'

A potential time bomb became my most intimate companion and it was only after years of regular CAT scans, and improved MRIs, that the location of the old bleed became more elusive. The neurologists believed that the malformation had sealed itself off, just as the neurologist said it might.

The tenth year after my CVA, I had an MRI.

The radiographer came in looking puzzled. 'Where is it, in the –?' He could only find what looked like a few crystals in the area where the old bleed had been.

TH, the neurologist, leant back in his chair and said with a cheeky grin, 'Anne, I hope never to see you again, at least, not under these circumstances. Whatever you're doing, keep on doing it.'

49

White Roses

About eighteen months after my stroke, I returned to porcelain painting. Before the stroke I'd run workshops on the latest decorating techniques. On the day of my stroke, I was applying freshly ground raised paste with a 000 brush onto a cartouche, on a small vase, which I'd ground ming blue, preparing samples for the course I was running which was on grounding, raised paste and gilding with different types of gold.

Now, my fine motor skills needed remediation. I decided a china painting workshop on Camellias would provide companionship and necessary remediation.

Workshop. A disaster but fellow painters are kind. 'Just think how far you've come.' My brushes do their best but after two days I throw a large plate covered in red blobs into the garbage bin. I listen to it smash.

I decided to go back to studies, this time by correspondence. I tried to enrol in English at New England University. The course was full but they suggested enrolling in Political Science, then in English the following year. They said they'd like more women to study politics. It was the last subject I ever wanted to study but accepted the offer because I was brain-hungry and needed to feed it if I was to get well. My husband and son came as carers when attending the residential.

I did lots of research on this unknown subject when preparing for a tutorial to be given at residential school. I read it aloud to the family for approval. They thought it was marvellous.

The tutor noted at the end of my delivery that most findings mentioned in the paper were based on Marxist theory and that should've been mentioned.

'Who's Marx?'

Fortunately, the tutor was sitting down.

I didn't finish the year in Politics; I dropped out in September, although I learnt a lot, and it did help feed my brain, but Marx (and/or was it Machiavelli?) proved to be too demanding of my attention. I couldn't justify giving their demands so turned my back on them, and on the politics of politics, and went back to the brush instead.

The brush moves freely but it's been over two years since the stroke. I'm convinced I'll never get my touch or eye back again. I have little confidence in myself although the brush is full of hope. My disappointment is ripe. Tears.

I have an idea. I ring my painting friend, F. I ask her if she'd like first offer to buy my fourteen-inch Ward kiln. I ask if she's interested in my sable brushes and the exquisite collection of yet-to-be-painted fine bone china. And is she interested in buying pats of unopened, unburnished gold? If she's not, then I'll put them up for sale.

Florence listens. 'I think that's a bad idea.' She suggests a full day's painting, once a fortnight, on the Central Coast. She'll ring the teacher. She's sure she'll squeeze me in although the class is full and has a long waiting list. She ignores protests and insists. 'It'll be a day out. Even if, to start with, you only come and eat a sandwich with us, it'll do you good.'

Once a fortnight, we sat at a long table in a glassed-in veranda, in the teacher's old cottage, couched in the luxurious grounds of the Fernery, which she and her husband owned. Spending a day painting with inspirational, gifted tutor, HD, delighting in a smorgasbord of learning and laughter, eating her gourmet sandwiches, lunching under the wisteria with chat and laughter, was delicious: soul food. I always came home with colour, brushstrokes, inspiration and laughter flowing freely in my veins.

Thanks to the persistence of my caring friend, my fine motor skills returned and beloved brushes responded accordingly. It was time for a challenge. White roses. White. Light. Shadows. Lavender. And although the porcelain felt heavy, its load was lightened by colour and sable song and I was painting again and firing.

After the CVA, the neurologist had warned me not to fall pregnant. 'It'd be too dangerous. You'd have to support another blood system… too much pressure. Get your husband to have the snip.'

But when my husband heard, he instinctively reached down and protected his treasure chest and shook his head. 'No way.'

Who would've thought that the challenge of painting white roses would pave the way for a miracle? Even today when I look at its light and shadow, I am reminded of the absolute joy in each brushstroke.

Falling pregnant at thirty-nine years of age was not an ideal time.

My GP said, 'If you go ahead with this, it's life-threatening. You have to consider the risk.'

I nodded. But this pregnancy seemed to have a quiet confidence of its own. Dr F rang the neurologist. He wanted back-up. Questions went back and forth. How could I tell them about the pumpkin dream?

I watch a flourishing pumpkin vine grow in the backyard. In the morning light, I see dewdrops on the voluminous green leaves which seem to be waltzing. Bees hover among brilliant yellow trumpets. I see one pumpkin, light-filled, fulsome, polished. I wake with its image still glowing and a knowing I'm going to have a baby girl.

When I'm fully awake, the more rational, sceptical part of me doubts it very much. Even after stroke recovery, with all logic and rational intention in place, the memory of the dream persisted. I convinced myself it was only wish fulfilment. It was a dream to let go.

My neurologist and GP chose a semi-retired obstetrician who dealt with complicated cases. Dr R was clever, kind and droll. On my first visit, he told me how often people who'd survived life-threatening events, such as stroke, fell pregnant. He said it could also affect the partner's fertility too. 'It's the body's way of recognising an urgent need to reproduce.' He said the most important thing for me now was to lead a quiet, uneventful life.

Early into the pregnancy, the schedules clerk was offered a

promotion in Sydney, a position he'd always wanted. After much discussion, he accepted the offer and I accepted the fact that my quiet life would come a little later. This move was intended to be long-term. We looked at the transfer back to Sydney as a positive, but to be taken with great care. We'd be near family at an exciting time. And, for me, once settled, I'd thrive on Sydney energy. After eleven years away, I looked forward to flying home with a strong tailwind. This seemed to be an answer to prayer.

The next few weeks were exhausting: preparing the house for sale, packing, moving. Our furniture would stay until settlement, hopefully, going straight into a new home. After the first open house, we had three offers. In the meantime, we moved to Sydney and settled, temporarily, in my old bedroom in Artarmon Road. We slept on the floor on a borrowed double-bed mattress.

I settled Paul into his new school at Artarmon and faced real estate agents and attended consultations with the clinically mannered obstetrician opposite the Royal North Shore Hospital, the hospital I once knew so well. We found a potential home in North Epping, close to schools and transport, with a lovely big bushy reserve out the back. I could see big family fun days out there. We paid the holding deposit but someone was very quiet.

'Is something wrong?'

In recent weeks, G had set off to work with a frown which grew deeper until it was a furrow. I thought I understood. He hated change. The move, like any move, was going to be difficult. I felt like frowning too. He said at work he was facing rapid changes in management. I understood. I was facing a few challenges myself.

He'd come home sullen, disappointed in the computerised, competitive office culture. Most working colleagues were university graduates, highly literate in computers. In Newcastle, he wasn't answerable to anyone, so the sale of the house was cancelled and we transferred back to Newcastle. I was so grateful for all the friends who rallied on our return.

Dr R, the obstetrician, stood at the end of the long corridor and beckoned. He smiled and nodded, looking satisfied at goodness-knows-what. He listened to the hows, whys and wherefores of the transfer. He shook his head. After the check-up, he suggested rest. 'You look like the Leaning Tower of Pisa. I know it hasn't toppled yet but by the look of you you're about to and we can't take that risk.' He suggested a week's rest in hospital.

The week of rest passed but he said to stay a little longer. It was New Year and my son was at home on school holidays but the doctor insisted. Everyone loved Paul. Generous neighbours and friends provided him with endless activities and sleepovers and, when I was feeling good, I asked to go home.

'We'll start with one day. Next Saturday.'

Saturday morning. Excited. I roll over and there's a landslide. Head spin, spin, spin. T, the neurologist, is away. A replacement finally arrives. He's obviously been dragged out of bed. He looks and smells like he's had a heavy night. He inspects my ears so roughly he causes one of them to bleed. He seems unaware how difficult it is for an almost ripe pumpkin to roll over and lie on its back with head hanging off the end of the bed. He swings it from side to side.

Vertigo goes wild. Can't see. Stemetil injection. Sides of the bed are put up. Spinning fast, praying for calm. 'Please, Lord, please don't let anything happen. We're so close.'

Home visits now out of the question. Options discussed. Baby's a good size. Caesarian moves forward a week.

In the meantime, I rested and walked, unaided, back and forth, back and forth, trying to detach myself from Fear. Occasionally Fear, in its greedy haste, almost knocked me over. But I was fortunate. There was an inner calm. I was learning to trust this inner calm which seemed to be anchored oceans deep.

From my room, I could see Newcastle ocean baths and the glorious stretch of the Pacific beyond. I was pleasantly surprised to see every morning that someone wrote 'Eternity' in the smooth sand, in copperplate script, similar to Arthur Stacey's *Eternity*, which he'd dedicated himself to write on the footpaths of Sydney for thirty-five years

My baby and I are part of eternity. Waves crash. We're part of the incoming tide. Tears. I'm overwhelmed; sheer gratitude for being at one in such an oasis of care and landscape. Thank you, Lord, thank you. I order extra food and blame the smell of salt water for the porky appetite. Could eat the menu. Extra food is stored in plastic containers in the side drawers so as not to share it with hungry mini-beasts; permanent residents.

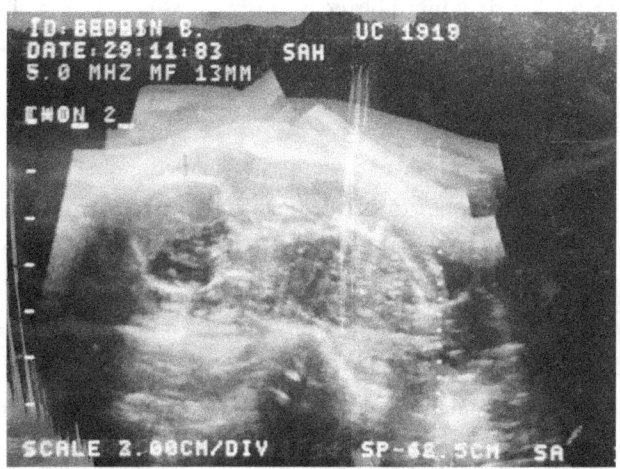

Rebecca – ultrasound, November 1993.

50
A Real Gem

My parents were due to arrive from Sydney in late January, soon after Ruby retired. She'd been overcome at her farewell dinner, just days before her sixty-ninth birthday. Business associates from all over Australia had gathered together to wish her well in her retirement. They stood, clapped and cheered this tiny woman who had quietly walked her way into their hearts.

Ten years earlier, when most of us had left home, Ruby was always looking for something useful to do. Marriage, children and grandchildren had brought her fulfilment but once her nest was empty she grew restless.

It used to be that sometimes, years ago, when I left for work, she'd stand in the front doorway and say, 'At least you've got something to look forward to, something you enjoy doing. I need to do something but I don't know what.'

I wished I could have taken her with me to school. She would've been invaluable in the classroom.

My sister, Wendy, had a heavy workload. It was so heavy that she'd sometimes bring hours of work home. She worked for a thriving photographic company which was in its infancy. Ruby would sit beside her at the table and she gradually learnt how to match negatives and edit photographs. So the obvious thing for her to do when extra staff were being recruited was for her to apply. She was known as 'the secretary's mum'. Ruby was always so quiet you'd be forgiven for not noticing her.

Twelve months later, the boss asked her to take charge of the reorder section. Ruby felt there were younger, capable workers who could do it but she was encouraged to accept the position. 'I'll do my best,' and she silently feared the written reports. She hated having to write anything such as memos for fear of making spelling mistakes. Before she sent one out, she'd flick through the well worn pages of her pocket dictionary, looking for the correct spelling.

It was her excellent memory which first came to their notice. She would be called to an occasional board meeting if there was any doubt about details. Soon, she attended all board meetings as a matter of course, her homespun wisdom often relied upon in the hurly-burly of takeovers and sabotage.

'Ask Ruby what she thinks,' came the catch cry from state to state. 'There's trouble in the lab…ask Ruby to go down.'

So while technology forged ahead in the late 70s and early 80s, Ruby, in her mid-sixties, nurtured, counselled and empowered her fellow workers as if they were family. By that time she was production manager at head office with a staff of twenty-four and was delighted to say she was the first woman to hold that position.

Looking out over the sea of smiling faces at her farewell dinner, Ruby thanked them for their friendship and loyalty. She told them she had another job. Stan, recently retired, needed full-time care and attention. He was too puffed out these days to put on his own shoes. Ruby knew that's where she wanted to be, and, on a brighter note, there was a new grandchild on the way.

Ruby and Stan.

51
Milk Tides

Early in the morning on 2 February, my young hairdresser friend arrived to cut my hair before she went to work. The unwieldy mop needed to be trimmed. After she left, I headed to the bathroom, intending to have a shower, but when I sat down my back muscles spasmed. Couldn't move. Rang the bell. Two nurses helped me back into bed.

'It feels like my spine has unzipped.'

The monitor was attached and it showed I was in first stages of labour. Nurses shaved and washed me and had difficulty getting rid of every fragment of freshly cut hair which I'd intended to wash away in the shower.

By late afternoon, family was by my side. I was due to go to theatre 9.30 p.m. The family followed me to the lift. As I was wheeled in, we looked at each other, and before the doors closed we drew in a communal breath. Would we see each other again? Except for my son, we all knew the risks. I just wished I could've taken the worry out of my parents' eyes.

When I was finally wheeled into theatre, it sounded like there was a party. I wished my family could've seen it. Neurologists, heart specialists, anaesthetists along with one or two curious, who'd asked for permission to be there, smiled. The atmosphere was like a celebration, like the moment before the cake's cut. Before I drifted off, I counted thirteen souls around the bed. We were in this together with every precaution being taken. God willing, soon there'd be another soul to join in the celebration.

Rebecca Anne Mary was born a strong, healthy baby at 9.55 p.m.

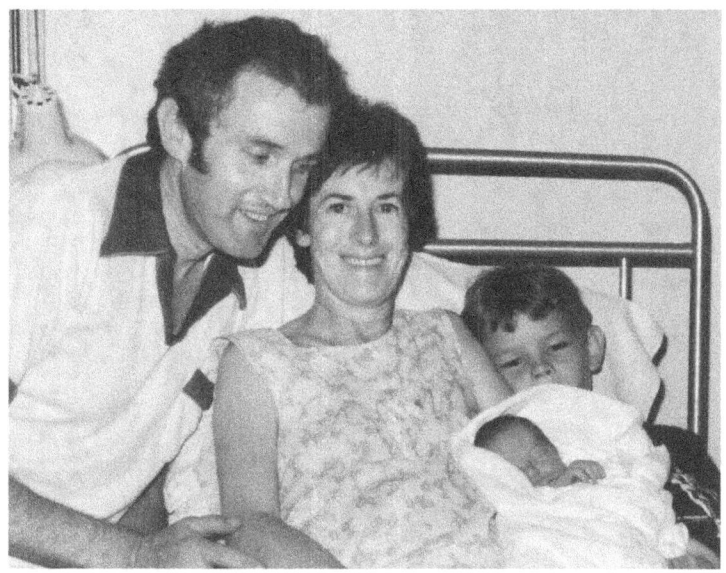
Graeme, Anne, Paul, Rebecca, 1984.

in the Royal Newcastle Hospital. Weight eight pounds. Height fifty-six centimetres.

In Recovery, they held her for me to see. I pulled a resistant eyelid open. Our daughter was swaddled in white. Only her face and hands were visible; a holy sight. I reached out and touched the tiniest, most elegant fingers and they curled around mine. 'You're so beautiful.' She was still powder-white from the womb and perfect. She looked like my childhood doll, Baby Doll: same profile, eyelashes, cheeks and Cupid mouth. And it wasn't a dream. We were both alive. Thank you, Lord, thank you.

Next morning I was wheeled back to my room, where a proud father, proud brother and proud grandparents and baby were waiting.

Stan said, 'I've never said so many Hail Marys in all my life. I'm surprised I could remember them.'

'Just as well,' I said.

On change-over of shifts, night and day sisters argued openly in front of mother and child. Day Sister insisted there'd be no need for supplements to be given at any time, day or night. Night Sister

*Graeme holding Rebecca, with Anne and Paul at home,
35 Valaud Crescent, Highfields.*

felt that a supplement was sometimes necessary. Day Sister said the mother's milk was coming in so should not be interfered with; that mother and baby had settled nicely. Night Sister said the obstetrician left instructions that the mother needed deep sleeps. Day Sister said the mother had at least two sound sleeps a day and that was sufficient.

One night I woke, reached out to touch Rebecca's crib. Where was it? I slipped out of bed, eyes half closed and headed for the nursery, managing to crash into the door on the way.

Sister heard the commotion and came running. 'She's fine. Back to bed…still a couple of hours till the next feed.'

It's day three. I sit by the window and stare, aware I'm also out there; part of a seismic shift; of being held, umbilically; a birthing star. Tears well. Senses on high alert. The earth breathes. The proud breast of ocean swells. I swell, too. Breasts fill; milk tides. I submit myself to the wondrous pull of life and weep and weep.

Word spread around the hospital about the miracle baby and mother. Interested doctors, family and friends visited. When it came time to leave, there were fond farewells and Day Sister looked pleased. She was probably relieved she could, once more, regain control of her floor.

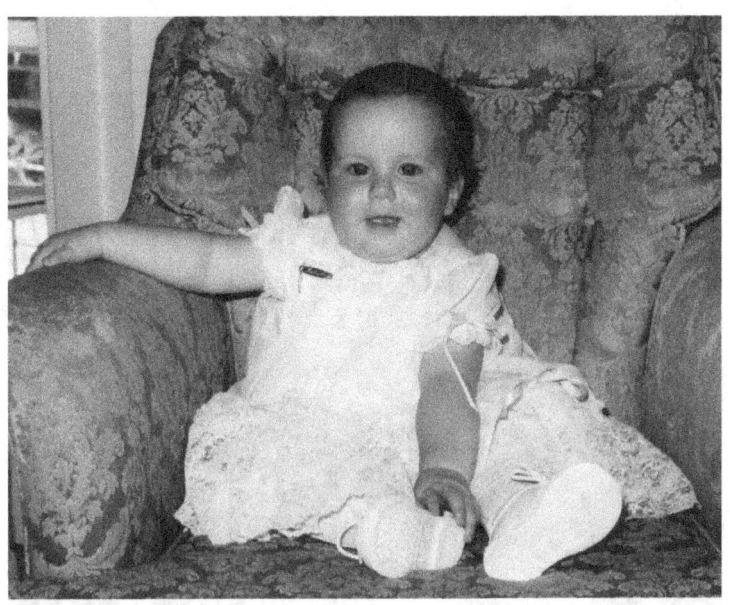

Rebecca Anne Mary.

In times past, I'd walked out of hospital with empty arms but this time I floated alongside proud father and son. They were loaded up with weeks of luggage and presents. I was grounded by arm-hugging gratitude for the small miracle in my arms. As we climbed into the car, I took a longing look across the road at the zinging blue of the ocean merging with the blue of the sky. There was no horizon to speak of, just the sound of destined waves arriving from distant shores where undercurrents moved unseen, obeying the ever-present pull of the moon.

Mr and Mrs Stanley Butt.

Family History and Influences

My maternal great-grandparents were Jack Thompson, born in 1864 in the ACT, and Annie Pearce, born in 1867 in Queanbeyan. For a time, Jack was a miner like his father. One of their children was my grandmother, Geraldine.

Geraldine was born at Captains Flat on 23 September 1896. On turning seventeen, it was arranged for her to travel to Sydney to work as a live-in maid for a wealthy Sydney family. Oral family history says even though Geraldine moved to the city, she managed to keep alive a romance with a local lad back home. When she fell pregnant, she corseted herself so tightly that no one at work knew she was with child. When the time was ripe, she returned home to give birth.

My mother, Myra Ruby Thompson, was born in Queanbeyan on 15 December 1914. Her grandmother, Annie (Gran), took immediate charge of her and the young mother was sent back to work. One would imagine she travelled back with aching arms and weeping breasts.

Ruby's understanding was that the young mother and father wanted to marry but were not allowed. When young, she remembered over-hearing that it had something to do with class or religion or, she said, 'It might've been both.' As an adult, Ruby felt she couldn't ask Gran who her father was because of all she'd done for her and she knew there was ill feeling between mother and daughter. In latter years, Ruby often wished she'd asked her mother about him; about them.

Geraldine met and married Edward Rose and gave birth to another daughter. Now that she was a respectable married woman, she expected to raise her eldest child but Annie refused to hand young Ruby back. Over the years, Geraldine persisted.

Ruby remembered a time when she was about ten years old. Aunt

Mr and Mrs Fred Butt.

Gell (Geraldine) arrived at the house one afternoon. There were raised voices. Gran shut the middle door. A younger cousin was staying. The young eavesdroppers lent over the balustrade and listened closely.

'I remember it as plain as day. Our house was always on the quiet side. Gran and Aunt Gell were shouting at each other. Gran was saying, "No, no, don't ever ask me again."

'Aunt Gell was crying so much that I thought something terrible had happened. She cried out, "But she's my daughter."

'My cousin turned and said, and I'll never forget it, "She's your mum." Of course, I didn't believe her. She said, "She is. My mum says so." I didn't know what to think. As far as I knew, Gran was my mother.'

Ruby started school in second grade. Until then, the family lived out of town on a farm with Gran's son, Will, who managed the farm. They lived with him and his wife, Nell, and their children. Will became Ruby's father figure over the years, a strong, much-loved gentleman.

They had regular family outings to and from town in horse and buggy. Oral history says that one Sunday when they were heading into town, the creek was up and running fast, so they prepared for a rough crossing. Gran sat holding a wicker basket of eggs. Family legend has it as they crossed the creek, the basket full of eggs flew into the air with Gran not far behind. She reached out, grabbed the basket and landed back on the sulky seat with a great thud and not one broken egg.

Ruby said that she could never warm to the parched days on the farm. She was thrilled when she learnt they were moving into town. While she'd miss her cousins and miss riding the old farm horse, she would never miss the isolation. 'It was so bare. So still. Some days I'd just sit there and look out over the paddock and hope that one blade of grass would move.'

Once in town, Ruby always found a reason to walk to and from the shops. She ran messages and did deliveries for Gran and a couple of her daughters, who ran a small pie shop in the main street of Yass. Ruby could walk to and from primary school and soon made friends, but, because of her late start, she was often behind in her schoolwork and wasn't allowed to play until she knew her spelling words. 'Teachers in those days were paid according to their successes.'

Ruby remembered standing in the blazing sun, watching steam rise off the asphalt while her friends played nearby. Even so, she loved school. She dreamt of becoming a teacher until she was taken out of school to help look after her cousin, Bill, who had scarlet fever. At the time, she was in sixth grade. It was accepted practice that young girls, especially young country girls, didn't need further education.

Nanna and Aunty.

Gran and Nanna Rose.

They were more useful at home. And Ruby was. Apart from helping nurse her cousin, another one of her duties was to help a neighbour's son who was ill with diabetes. She had to regularly give him insulin injections in his stomach.

Caring for others and for animals was not unusual. Ruby was used to watching Gran tend to and care for someone else or some injured animal. Gran was considered, by some, to be the unofficial vet until one moved into town, because she had a healing way with animals.

Ruby shared a double bed with Gran and had memories of spending many nights with a sick animal lying between them. Patients would be swaddled in clean cloths and placed on heated salt packs and tucked into a small box or a cane basket. Gran's chirp-chirp-chirping and cluck-cluck-clucking settled the patient and put her granddaughter to sleep.

1929. Australia's economy suffered a severe downturn. Wall Street crashed in October that year and Australia entered a worldwide Great Depression which lasted until 1932. Jobs were scarce.

It was in February 1930 when Ruby was sent to the city to work. It was commonplace for country girls to live in at their place of employment. She was a sensible sixteen-year-old and went to live with a family who owned a shop with the residence above. Ruby cared for the young children and was also expected to work in the shop with the owner. Unfortunately, the owner was more interested in pursuing the young woman around the counter, so she left almost as soon as she started.

Alternative accommodation was organised with an aunt and uncle who'd recently moved into a small cottage in Queen Street, Woollahra. It was decided that Ruby would stay with them until Gran moved to the city.

She found work in a laundry at Double Bay. It was hot, heavy work but she was young and strong. She'd set out early of a morning and enjoyed the long walk: the bay, parks and gardens. Ruby was a city girl at heart. 'I was so happy my feet hardly touched the ground. I only ever noticed the long walk home at the end of an extra long day.'

Steam rose and parched Ruby's throat while the Depression parched the souls of the unemployed outside. She worked in the laundry for almost ten years, eventually becoming a head presser, which meant a few extra pennies of pay, which meant she could afford to buy material to make a new dress.

Ruby loved ballroom dancing. Occasionally, she entered competitions with a dance partner at the Trocadero and Paddington Town Hall. Sometimes she could afford to go ice-skating. On Saturday afternoons, she played vigro with workmates.

One of her workmates, Nellie Butt, was having an engagement party at North Sydney. Nellie joked that she had a couple of unmarried brothers and she'd pair Ruby off with her brother, Reg. 'You'll make good dance partners. Ollie can have Stan.'

As the story goes, Stan had other ideas. 'The first time I laid eyes on your mother, I saw this mop of thick, wavy hair. She had the best pair of legs in the room. I was over there like a shot.'

'And we danced every dance.'

'Too right.'

And their dance lasted fifty-five years till death did them part.

'When I met your father, I thought someone like him would never be interested in the likes of me. He was tall, dark and handsome. The girls at work used to call him Jimmy Stewart. I thought he'd never come all the way from North Sydney to see me. I was always a bit surprised when he turned up.'

Stanley Butt was born on 1 December 1915 at Crows Nest. He was the fifth of six children and lived with his parents, four brothers, an older sister and two younger cousins who were raised like sisters.

Stan's mother, Caroline Maude Salter, was born in Islington, London, on 30 September 1877. At that time, Australia was considered a frontier country. By the time Caroline turned twenty, she'd been influenced by the many advertisements about Australia needing young women to come and help build a strong nation. And, more importantly, there was promise of employment. It sounded like Utopia compared to the current conditions in England.

Caroline's parents were aghast at their daughter's intention to emigrate. They forbade her to go. It was unthinkable that a daughter of theirs would even consider setting sail with the intention of settling in a colony full of bootleggers and convicts. They warned her that if she went, she'd be disowned.

The closely chaperoned young emigrants set sail for Australia on the Duke of Norfolk. Caroline's good friend/cousin, Charlotte, disembarked in Townsville and Caroline disembarked in Brisbane, in February 1901, just one month after Australia's first Constitution was enacted. In two more years, white Australian women would be allowed to vote and stand as members of Federal Parliament. That would not happen in the Mother Country until the late 1920s. The excited young adventurer was willingly swept up in the fast-flowing current that was shaping the young nation.

Caroline's first position was as a nanny. One morning when she was taking her charge for a walk, a fellow followed her into the park, calling out lewd remarks and making rude gestures. 'I could see in the distance there was this tall, young man coming the other way. I didn't know if he might stop and help. I was ever so thankful when he did. He asked me if the fellow was pestering me. He soon told him to be off in no uncertain terms.'

The tall, young man was Frederick Butt. He'd recently come ashore in Brisbane after a brief time in the Merchant Navy, which he disliked. He much preferred working on the land. When Caroline thanked him for his knightly deed, he recognised her English accent. His father's family had emigrated from Dorset and her father was from Devon.

'From that moment on, we never stopped talking: politics, poetry, philosophy. It was not until the day he died did we stop talking. In spite of everything, I loved him. He was my soulmate.'

Frederick's father's family emigrated from Dorset in the mid-1880s. They worked on his uncle's sheep station in the Yass area. After Frederick senior's first wife died, he married Eleanor Payne. He had several children and Frederick junior was the only child of their union. Frederick junior was born on 16 October 1877 at Bowning Creek, Yass. The Butt children were well educated for those times. Fred's step-siblings chose to go into professions but Fred junior had other inclinations. He much preferred the outdoors and working on the land.

From an early age, it was said, he expressed strong socialist leanings. His political idealism embarrassed his family. But it was not unusual in those days to be influenced by free thinkers and persuasive speakers who were trying to cut the Mother Country's umbilical cord. Fred left home in the 1890s when there was talk of forming an Australian Utopia in Paraguay. At the same time, the Communist Party was attracting thinkers and philosophers alike, and it was showing signs of promise, espousing socialist ideals.

Fred was an experienced horseman. On one of his droving trips in western New South Wales, sometime between 1892 and 1893, he met a young man, Henry Lawson, who'd been commissioned by the *Bulletin* to look at, and report back on, the conditions that drovers, stockman and shearers endured. It would be years later that Fred would show his young sons Lawson's published works and tell them how this cobber knew what he was talking about. He was writing about him, Fred, and about men like him, who told this young cove their grim stories of drought, hunger and hardship.

Frederick Butt and Caroline Salter married at St Thomas Church of England, North Sydney, on 22 March 1905. They settled in Crows Nest because Caroline felt at home there. It reminded her so much of England.

At one stage, Fred worked for the council and he also worked as a timber carrier. It was pre-Harbour Bridge days and North Sydney had an important timber mill on the harbour's edge, mainly for maritime purposes. It also provided timber for new cottages which were being built in North Sydney, which, at the time, was experiencing a surge in population.

After many years of hauling timber, Fred had an accident at work and was badly injured. Much to his shame, Caroline became the sole provider. She found work as a full-time laundress in Wollstonecraft.

By now, Fred was an invalid and sadly became an alcoholic. He spent many days in North Sydney pubs. It was where he met up again with Henry L. Invalids, alcoholics, damaged men, dreamers, philosophers all, would talk and drink themselves legless. Sometimes Fred would come home angry and frustrated with his lot and take aim at his wife or one of the children.

Stan often said, 'That's one thing I can thank the old bastard for. He taught me how not to treat your wife and kids.'

'Stan,' Ruby would say, 'that's your father you're talking about. That's not a nice thing to say. When he was sober, he was a lovely man. Always had something interesting to say and he really was a gentleman. It was the alcohol –'

Fred and Caroline were avid readers. After Fred's death, Caroline kept many of his books, some of which were copies of Lawson's books, well-worn copies of *The Bulletin*, and most of C.J. Dennis's work, much of which Fred knew by heart, as did his youngest sons, Stan and Arthur. They were the ones who read or recited to him.

Stan said, 'We never squibbed. Reading or reciting to him was the quickest way to calm the old bastard down.'

Those books from which he read were passed down to Stan. Caroline knew they contained much of her husband's spirit and his son then shared them with us.

In a copy of Lawson's *In the days when the world was wide and other verses*, Fred wrote in 1913, in beautiful script, small pieces of verse.

Thomas Moore, 'Paradise & the Peri' (1779–1852)

Poor race of men!
said the pitying Spirit,
Dearly ye pay for your primal Fall.
some flowers of Eden
ye still inherit –

but the trail of the
serpent is over them all.

And verse from

> George Linnaeus Banks (1821–1881)
>
> For the cause that lacks assistance –
> the wrong that needs resistance –
> for the future in the distance –
> and the good that I can do.

Fred was Catholic and Caroline was Protestant. The children attended the nearby Catholic school, St Leonards, at Naremburn. Now that their mother was working full-time, Nellie, the eldest daughter, took on before and after school care of siblings. The nuns helped. They often minded the younger children so Nellie could attend class.

Fred was not a practising Catholic and would not allow his children to attend regular Mass or Confession, but he gave them permission to take First Communion. They adopted a saint's name. For many years, I believed my father's full name was Stanley Francis Butt.

Fred and Caroline's two youngest sons were said to be very bright. They topped classes in arithmetic and English. In those days, there was no free high school education, so the Sisters offered to keep Stan on at school. Soon his younger brother, Arthur, caught up with him. They were allowed to stay on for another couple of years, with free access to the school's limited resources and a small library.

'Sometimes, we had to help some joker out with his sums,' Stan said.

Meanwhile, the Sisters extended these gifted boys in mathematics and English. Stan often wondered aloud about the privilege. It was as if he couldn't believe it. The selfless nuns gave him a lifelong love of independent learning. How he would've loved the Internet!

Unlike Ruby, Stan's work during the years of the Great Depression was piecemeal. Two of his older brothers were apprentice barbers in Crows Nest. Stan asked if there was any work for him but the owner had already taken on one apprentice too many.

When Stan first met Ruby, he was working in a dry cleaner's. It was an improvement on his last job, where he'd worked on a cattle station out of Griffith. The cruelty of castrating animals stayed with him for life. 'We had to kick them down, grab their balls and cut them off, just like that. No beg pardons. Poor buggers. You'd hear them howling.'

Unfortunately for Stan, he was allergic to dry cleaning chemicals. Skin peeled off his hands, even with gloves, and they became infected. He had no choice but to leave.

Early one morning, when it was still dark, he set out in his older brother's good shoes because they were the only ones in the house that had decent soles. Stan had a long walk ahead of him. He was following up talk about a job near Parramatta. He waited, in a long, hungry queue and put his name down. He arrived back late at night and by then his brother had discovered his good shoes were missing. The shoes were inspected. There were words and Stanley had to pay to have the shoes resoled. 'And I didn't get the bloody job.'

His next job was delivering milk on Sydney's northern beaches. It was too far to travel each day so he boarded out the back of the Boss's place during the week. As with many businesses, his boss was having difficulty paying wages. Often during this time Stan wrote to Ruby.

'I don't know when I am going to be paid because the boss is broke to the world. She hasn't even got enough money to pay for all the milk...I suppose you are working pretty late of a night now. I hope to cripes you haven't got to work as late as you did last year. I pity you if you have to, that was bad enough to knock anyone out. Well, Rube, I have been up since 3 o'clock this morning and it is 9 o'clock (p.m.) now so I think I will close up for now and say good night.'

With little or no pay, Stan decided to leave the horse and cart behind. He expected trouble from his mother for quitting but it wasn't long before he sat for an entrance exam in maths and English with the State Railways and Tramways Institute. He was called in for a further interview and offered a job in the office. Stan wasn't expecting that. A white-collar job? 'I couldn't come at that. Couldn't see muggins here sitting cooped up at a desk all day.' So he accepted the next best offer, tram conductor. 'Your old man already knew how to ride a running board. You can thank your mother for that.'

During the five years of Stan and Ruby's courtship, Stan rode many running boards, unofficially of course. He rarely had enough money for a fare. Often there were razor gang spikes: stabbings and killings when trouble brewed between rival gangs of drugs and sly grog. If Stan didn't have the fare at those times, Ruby would press a coin into his hand and make him promise to catch trams all the way home. 'If there was real trouble, I'd catch them…not worth being cut for a measly penny. Cripes, if I hadn't, I'd never have heard the end of it from your mother.'

The young couple's courtship was tested by Gran's determination to stop her Protestant granddaughter going out with a Catholic. But Ruby was every bit as determined as her grandmother. Unbeknownst to Gran, the two would meet at Uncle Will and Aunty Nell's place, which was just a few miles away at Moore Park. Ruby would make some excuse and say she was spending the day sewing with her cousins. These were the same cousins Ruby had lived with on the farm when very young.

Some weekends, Stan and Ruby would pool their pennies with friends and hire a car and go for drives: Three Sisters, Katoomba; Wentworth Falls; Northern Beaches; Nielsen Park; West Head; North Head. They'd walk to Bondi, look at the well-dressed windows in David Jones and Mark Foys, which mirrored their hopes.

Sometimes, they and their friends would hire a tennis court, rackets and balls and make up their own competition. In season, on Saturday afternoons, both Ruby and Stan played sport. Ruby played vigro at Moore Park and Stan played cricket on North Sydney Oval. Saturday nights they went dancing or to the pictures.

On Sunday nights, it was always baked dinner at the Butts. Any newcomers were quickly initiated. Ruby had never experienced anything like the shenanigans that went on around the large mahogany table that could sit ten if need be. The siblings would tell jokes and play games, many of which tested the newcomer.

Ruby thrived on Butt family's *joie de vivre* and wit but it was difficult for her to visit them regularly without Gran's knowledge. Uncle Will intervened on the young couple's behalf. He spoke to Mother, who grudgingly agreed. 'But,' said Stan, 'it was the same old. If I stuck my head in the joint, it was pistols at fifty paces.'

After years of a festering power struggle in Europe, Germany invaded Poland. It proved to be one invasion too many. Great Britain declared war on Germany in September 1939, and the mother country would rely on strong, young Australians to volunteer for active service.

Stan always failed the medical because of his high insteps. Each time, after another sibling was accepted in the armed forces, he'd try again. Finally, he received notification that he was required for essential services. It was time to stop pestering the local recruitment officer.

In such uncertain times, Stan's public service employment was equal to blue ribbon investment so he proposed to Ruby. At first, his mother was upset. There was a war on and Caroline was looking forward to some financial relief at home but, at heart, she was a generous, selfless soul and gave them her blessing.

Meanwhile, Gran ran a tea house in the front room of her rented Paddington terrace. She took in ironing but there was not enough money to pay for a wedding, and besides, the effects of the war had subdued most celebrations. Even so, after a five-year courtship, Stan and Ruby married at All Saints, Woollahra, on 20 April 1940. They paid for the wedding themselves and, in spite of family fear-mongers saying they couldn't afford to marry, they were proud of the fact that, after all expenses were paid, they were still in credit. 'We started out with five pounds in the bank.'

The young couple packed a port full of dreams and, more importantly, travelled in the same direction for the next fifty years.

After renting an unsuitable small bungalow in Willoughby, the newly-weds moved into a three-bedroom Federation brick bungalow, 68 Penshurst Street, Willoughby. Gran moved in with them three weeks later and 68 soon became the busy hub for extended family and friends.

When their firstborn, Robert Stanley, arrived nine months and one week after the wedding, an aunt whispered in Ruby's ear how pleased she was that she'd been discreet enough to wait a week but she should've waited a little longer so as not to be seen to be in such a hurry.

Stan was punctilious about time, an essential attribute for anyone working to a timetable. He set every clock in the house ten minutes early and could tell the correct time without the help of the sun or his watch. But he was notoriously difficult to wake of a morning because of his lifelong late-night reading habit. Regardless of an early start, Stan would read well past the end of the day. He was one of the most voracious borrowers of the private lending library, three doors down from 68, owned and run by Mr O'Dowd, a well educated South African gentlemen.

Ruby was a sound sleeper. She could fall asleep mid-sentence. She often woke in the early hours to find her neck hot from the heat of the big reading lamp perched high in the middle of their wooden bedhead. She'd remind Stan to turn off the light or he'd never get up in the morning.

She'd rise early. Even before Stan had opened his eyes, he could smell hot black tea and thick coating of dripping with its generous sprinkling of salt and pepper on hot slices of toast, placed on the middle shelf of his smoker's stand. 'Stan, Stan, wake up.' He'd prop himself up on one elbow, sip his strong black tea, roll a Ruby Red and blow smoke signals into the new day.

And it worked both ways. 'I don't know what I would've done without your father. If it was a Monday and he happened to have a long morning break, he'd help with the washing. He never liked the idea of me lifting heavy, wet washing out of the copper and into the tub. He'd insist on doing it if he was around. He'd put it through the ringer while I hung out clothes. He never complained, you know.'

Stan was a SNAG (sensitive new age guy) at heart, long before such an acronym existed.

Around the time of my birth, Ruby was looking after two young sons: a three-year-old Robert and a much more demanding eighteen-month-old, Lennie. In addition, she cooked and cared for an assortment of adults.

68 Penshurst Street functioned like a rhizome. If there was a problem, it was a case of 'Ask Stan and Rube',which usually resulted in 68 sprouting another lateral shoot: a relative or friend from either side of the family who'd stay for weeks, months and, in some cases, years.

Uncle Mick, Gran's eldest son, a returned Gallipoli Light Horseman, was a bachelor and became so ill he moved into 68 to be nearer Mother. He was a respectful presence and slept in the semi-enclosed back veranda, a permanent resident until his death many years later.

At other times, Stan's maternal Aunty Nellie (Aunty) stayed intermittently at 68, sharing a bedroom with Gran. Aunty was a midwife who sometimes lived in with families to provide before and after care for mother and child. But by the time I was to be born, she'd retired with her sister, Nanna, who was now widowed. They lived together at Hazelbrook in the Blue Mountains.

One day, Uncle Bill arrived on the back doorstep of 68 with a lightly packed port and two army issue blankets under his arm. He was one of the many damaged survivors of the Japanese prisoner of war camps. Gran had raised Bill as good as a son. 'You can't turn him away,' she said, 'not after all he's been through.' So Bill took up residence on the back veranda of 68, sleeping on a small single bed at the foot of his uncle's bed.

Ruby and Stan's firstborn, Robert Stanley, was a good eater, calm in nature and a good sleeper. Two years later, Leonard Arthur was born and couldn't have been more different. He was a fussy eater and didn't need much sleep. About three of a morning he'd wake and stand up at the end of his cot at the end of his parents' bed and perform impromptu concerts. His exhausted parents couldn't help but laugh. When Lenny was eighteen months old, he was promoted into a big boy's bed in his big brother's bedroom. The cot needed a fresh coat of paint before the new baby arrived.

Ruby and Stan, always dancing.

www.ingramcontent.com/pod-product-compliance
Lightning Source LLC
Chambersburg PA
CBHW071811080526
44589CB00012B/756